The Winter of
Our Discount Tent

THE WINTER OF OUR DISCOUNT TENT

A Humorous Look at Flora, Fauna, and Foolishness Outdoors

by Jim Mize

University of South Carolina Press

Text and jacket illustrations by Cliff Shelby

Copyright © 1995 University of South Carolina

Published in Columbia, South Carolina by the
University of South Carolina Press

Manufactured in the United States of America

Library of Congress Cataloging-in-Publication Data

Mize, Jim, 1953–
    The winter of our discount tent : a humorous look at flora, fauna, and
foolishness outdoors / Jim Mize.
        p.   cm.
    ISBN 1-57003-049-9
    1. Natural history—Miscellanea. 2. Natural history—Humor.
I. Title.
QH45.5.M58 1995
508—dc20   94–18752

For the codgers who
took me afield when I was young
and made me laugh.

Contents

continued. . .

Preface

My editor suggested that *The Winter of Our Discount Tent* would be the ideal book to keep in your bathroom. Remembering the fate that struck the Sears catalog where I grew up, I asked her to elaborate.

"It's the sort of book," she explained, "that is best read in short sittings."

A good point, but there are countless other times and places this book could be read, such as on planes or subways, before bed or during lunch, on rainy camping trips or late nights at the beach. You see, the recipe for this book called for it to be a dessert, full and satisfying, leaving a good taste in your mouth, but maybe too rich to be consumed all at once.

So if you decide this is the ideal book for your bathroom, I can live with that. But please, this is no Sears catalog.

Acknowledgments

Most books that finally make it into print are the result of many people working toward a single goal. This one is no exception.

Linda Renshaw, who edited this book, deserves credit for knowing the difference between polishing and reconstructive surgery.

Cliff Shelby's illustrations added color to my verbal images.

A number of these articles appeared in other publications, and in many cases, improved by having that publication's editor offer his or her input on an earlier draft. Among the publications whose editors deserve thanks are: *South Carolina Wildlife, North American Whitetail, South Carolina Game & Fish, Blue Ridge Outdoors, Carolina Adventure, The Varmint Hunter Magazine, Trophy Striper, Wildlife in North Carolina, Canoe, California Angler, Pennsylvania Angler,* and *Field & Stream.*

Finally, any family who lives in the same house with a humorist has to play multiple roles. They represent the front line of defense for bad jokes. They constantly serve as subject matter, and any mishap is rewarded by public exposure. And they also make sacrifices while the humorist sits at a computer recording for other people something that will hopefully spark a chuckle. So for their scrutiny of my jokes, their comical tendencies, and their patience, my thanks go to Jan, Corey, and Stuart.

The Winter of
Our Discount Tent

Weeds
Gone Bad

Kudzundheit!

Radio stations don't carry kudzu reports for two simple reasons. First, the rate of spread would scare small children into a lifetime fear of houseplants. Second, announcers would have to update their reports on the hour. Kudzu grows so fast that many people believe that if you stand very still, you can see it happen. Most of these people are now missing.

As you might have noticed, kudzu fields are always full of lumps. It makes you wonder. Botanists note that one kudzu vine in a single season can grow one hundred feet. The only problem is that there's no such thing as *one* kudzu vine.

These same botanists point out that the root alone has been known to weigh as much as four hundred pounds, when you can stop one long enough to weigh it.

With kudzu taking over much of the South and making plans to ambush your yard, you might wonder where it came from. And you probably figured, the answer, as with many other imports, is JAPAN! Kudzu was first brought to the United States from the Orient in 1876. In fact, the word kudzu is thought to translate from Japanese, "the joke's on you." Unfortunately, in 1876, few Americans spoke Japanese.

During the early years after its introduction, kudzu was viewed as a miracle plant, gaining fame and support. To give you an example, in the late 1930s and 1940s, the federal government was recommending planting kudzu, in some cases subsidizing the cost by as much as $8 per acre. The Civilian Conservation Corps even helped plant it. Their goal was to turn the dust bowl into a salad bowl.

In South Carolina, R. Y. "Kudzu" Bailey, an agronomist with the Soil Conservation Service in Spartanburg, is credited or blamed with writing the first comprehensive booklet on kudzu. He no doubt considered it a lively topic that could never be fully covered.

At this time, people even sold kudzu by mail order. Most of them have now been paroled.

With all this support, kudzu soon became so popular that it had its own club, including 20,000 members and branches everywhere. Georgia even elected a kudzu queen, a tall, slim girl.

Florida claims the honor of beginning the spread of kudzu in the South, naming Chipley the Kudzu Capital. Any town that mass-cultivated kudzu would also have made a good site for an Edsel factory.

Stories about kudzu abound. Some historians believe that Jack's beanstalk was actually kudzu. I doubt it, though, since the tale never mentions Jack's house being near a power line.

Before you get the impression that kudzu is a worthless menace, however, let me point out its multiple uses.

For starters, you can eat it. Just don't close your eyes when you bow for grace.

Kudzu powder, made from dried and ground kudzu roots, can be used to thicken soup or coat foods for deep-frying. It is especially useful when company drops in unexpectedly and you have extra mouths to feed. Just let it simmer a bit longer to stretch the meal. Plan on about thirty minutes per extra hundred people.

Kudzu-cooking requires special instructions, including tips such as, "Don't turn your back on it!"

Kudzu noodles are popular with kids, especially when they discover that, by putting one end of a kudzu noodle in their mouths and slurping, they can inhale their whole dinner.

Scientists recently began genetics research on kudzu to improve its food value. One has crossed it with tomatoes. Not only is the resulting hybrid prolific, but by the time the fruit's ripe it's at your door.

Hardy and fast-growing, kudzu may be considered a likely plant for space colonies. Of course, planting kudzu in space would flush out once and for all any aliens that might be there, and who knows how they would retaliate. Scientists believe, however, that kudzu could be controlled by planting it only on one planet. This might work, provided the planets were never connected by power lines.

The other potential uses for kudzu are numerous. It could be used for erosion control, livestock fodder, ornamental decorations, or hiding your neighbors' house as a prank while they're on vacation.

Farmers considering feeding it to livestock might want to know that the county extension recommends no more than ten cows per acre of kudzu. That's about all the cattle it can eat.

In Japan, kudzu vines are even woven into fabric for clothes, giving new meaning to the term "Active Wear."

Some people attribute kudzu with medicinal benefits, including the ability to cure intestinal disorders, colds, fevers, and hangovers. No definitive evidence exists on its curative powers, but I interviewed several sources who claimed it had driven them to drink.

Kudzu does have some unusual uses. For instance, its fibers have been used to stuff cushions, beds, and chairs. Home mattress kits can be mailed in an eight-by-ten-inch Spandex envelope. By the time it arrives, it's a king-size Posturepedic.

Quail hunters also figure out quickly that not only is a kudzu field a good place to hunt birds, but later in the day, it's also a good place to hunt your dog, particularly if he's steady on point. Just watch for the kudzu lump that moves after you yell, "Hunt on!"

Kudzu, as all survivors know, can create some real problems. Telephone companies have trouble with the weight of kudzu pulling down poles. Electrical companies complain about it shorting out transformers. And rural road crews blame kudzu for the annual loss of at least three road scrapers.

Just walking in a field of kudzu can be dangerous. In fact, you can't always be sure there's a field under you. Were seeds sprinkled over the Grand Canyon this fall, by next spring some hiker would take one very long step just after asking his partner, "Did you hear water?"

Now that kudzu has been reclassified by many as an undesirable plant, much effort has gone into eliminating it. Scientists have learned numerous ways to get rid of kudzu, but the most effective is still to sell your property and move to Saskatoon.

One of the better methods of eradicating kudzu is to stock the field with pigs. Not only do they dig up the roots, but they also will make every effort to consume the vines. Of course, should your kudzu have already reached the telephone line, you will either need to train your pigs on high wires or put up signs warning, "Watch For Falling Pigs."

You can see that kudzu is nothing to sneeze at. But if you do, don't forget to say, "Kudzundheit."

Plants You Can Eat

For starters, let me explain that all plants are edible. It's just that some of them will kill you.

Perhaps a more precise title for this chapter would have been "Plants You Can Eat And Not Die." While I was researching the topic, at least one person asked if this category included broccoli.

The idea of walking into the woods, digging up plants, and eating them always intrigued me. This practice started long before scientists could point at plants and recommend warning labels. In fact, the first wild-plant eaters were probably desperate people who figured it out by trial and error. No doubt, they were very polite people.

"No, Ethel, you were here first. Go ahead and eat that flowering thing there."

"No, no, no. I wouldn't think of it, Claud. You go right ahead. I know you must be famished."

Sooner or later, they would compromise and eat at the same time. For some reason, I picture the prehistoric forests as being littered with really sick people.

This early problem of sorting through all the plants to determine which ones were edible may also explain why God gave us little brothers. "Give it to Mikey" was a practice that certainly began before the cereal companies thought of it.

And not all edible plants look like something you'd eat. Take mushrooms. The guy who discovered they were edible was probably also the first to try raw oysters and escargot.

Nowadays, a number of edible plants are well-known, such as blackberries, blueberries, and walnuts. Most people recognize them

5

by the green baskets they come in and may be surprised to learn they grow on vines, bushes, and trees.

Other plants, however, are considerably more obscure. These have names like snake root, skunk cabbage, and motherwort. Even if they tasted good, you can see why they don't show up on restaurant menus.

This question of taste raises another interesting point. Just saying a plant is edible lacks accuracy. For instance, I can think of at least three categories of edibility. The first I would describe as "This plant won't kill you." All the ingredients of castor oil fit this category.

The second is "This doesn't taste half bad." Cardboard would be a good example if it grew wild.

Third, there's the category of "Plants you would eat twice." To me, these are the only ones that matter, and they usually show up in green baskets at your supermarket.

The best way to be introduced to edible plants is by a knowledgeable friend, preferably one without a sense of humor. Unfortunately, my introduction was by the other kind of friend, a title that was later reduced considerably.

Except for berries and nuts, I had never eaten wild plants until Scooby introduced me to ramps. We were in a dry hollow estimating timber volumes one day when Scooby spied the ramp. At the time, the only ramps I was familiar with were boat ramps, which, as it turns out, are equally edible.

A ramp looks like a cross between a lily and a turnip and tastes like a cross between horseradish and cayenne peppers. Immediately upon swallowing that first bite, miles from drinking water, I was struck by a fire in my throat that would have summoned Smokey Bear if I hadn't been sucking wind so hard that none of the smoke got out. Talk about thirst. At that precise moment, I'd have paid ten dollars just to lick the dew off the windshield of a pulpwood truck.

I practically stampeded Scooby as I fled the woods, then drove four miles to a country store and downed two RC Colas, just so I could regain my voice and appropriately thank Scooby, much to the embarrassment of the store owner.

Not all wild plants are consumed for food; some are sought for their medicinal value. Probably the most famous of these is ginseng. A few years ago a ginseng craze swept the nation, and you could buy ginseng pills, ginseng tea, and even ginseng lotions. About the only thing you couldn't get was a good reason for buying it.

Originally, most ginseng was exported to the Far East where it was thought to be an aphrodisiac. Later, scientists showed it actually stimulates the digestive tract and works as a mild laxative. This could mean that the next controversial issue to hit our school systems will be the regulation and distribution of Ex-Lax.

Ginseng is a rare plant that grows wild from Georgia to Canada, especially in the eastern mountain ranges. Until you actually find some, its leaf is easily mistaken for other wild plants. For instance, one of my buddies went into the ginseng business and accidentally dug poison oak roots until he had $40 worth. At least, that's what the doctor's bill came to.

Many plants found in the wild are incorporated into home remedies. At one time, most of these tonics were manufactured in large batches using an alcohol base with corn the primary ingredient. The government later frowned upon many of these recipes.

Outdoorsmen often operate under the notion that when all else fails, they have the wherewithal to live off the land. This is another one of those ideas that sound better in theory than in practice. What are the odds you would be lost, stranded, or trying to survive within sight of blackberries during the two weeks they are ripening? That leaves fifty weeks and a multitude of other locations where plant identification could be critical.

Then how does an outdoorsman determine which plants are edible? One possibility is to wait for an animal to come along eating plants and then just eat what it eats. I have a better idea. Why not eat the animal?

And then there are the other aspects to this edible-plant issue, such as collecting and preparing the plants. In my experience this can be so time consuming that by the time you're done, you could have walked to McDonald's and ordered a Big Mac.

That's why for the average guy, wild plants are more likely table conversation than table fare.

Which brings us back to that earlier question I received about whether or not broccoli is edible. Yes, Mr. Bush, it is. I'm not sure, however, about that little parsley sprig restaurateurs keep putting on my plate. I'll let you know as soon as I see somebody else eat one.

Plants That Can Eat You

"Carnivorous plants." Just thinking about them conjures up images of elephants in Tarzan films being devoured by foot-sucking plants. Of course, I realize this is ridiculous. Everyone knows that elephants aren't good to eat.

Carnivorous plants are a real quirk of nature. Basically, they are plants that eat animals. No doubt they have triggered the imaginations of many, probably including the guy who invented stuffed peppers.

Most carnivorous plants eat insects. Some even feed on slugs, probably because they can outrun them. The largest known species of carnivorous plants can catch and devour birds and rodents. Since these plants never need a litter box, in my mind this puts them several notches above cats. Besides, none of *them* will ever cough up a hair ball.

Carnivorous plants usually grow in habitats poor in minerals, getting what they need by consuming insects. Put another way, ideal habitat for a carnivorous plant would be my truck windshield.

Scientists postulate that we have not yet discovered all the carnivorous plants, something to remember as you walk your dog.

Some people actually collect carnivorous plants, though for some unexplained reason, there seems to be fewer and fewer of them. Clubs have even formed with the primary purpose of trading carnivorous plants. Just think, they could not only bring their plants to the meetings, but could also take them out afterward for a bite.

Carnivorous plants trap insects in different ways. Some use pitfalls or funnels that lead insects into a trap. Others use adhesive, like flypaper. Still others actually snap shut to grab the insect. Under no instance, however, are any known to use RAID. That's probably because of the aftertaste.

The best-known carnivorous plant is Venus' fly trap. These plants actually snap shut when an insect wanders inside and triggers the hairs that close the trap. This all happens so fast, you barely have time to hear them yell, "Gotcha!"

When I was a kid, I had a Venus' fly trap. I remember I used to hunt bugs just to feed it. I often wonder if it trained me to do that.

The fly trap's native habitat is within a 100-mile radius of Wilmington, North Carolina. Its territory would have been larger, but it just wasn't that hungry.

When botanists go afield, I can imagine them telling Venus' fly trap jokes. They probably go something like this: "Did you hear the one about the fly trap that went out to eat but ended up sending its food back, complaining 'Hey, waiter, there's no fly in my soup!' "

Lesser-known plants like the sundew also eat insects. In fact, these plants have large appetites. Some have been found eating up to a hundred insects at a time, each one captured individually. Can you imagine how frustrated a little sundew's mother must get trying to teach it not to chew with its mouth full?

Sundews catch insects by attracting them to sticky tentacles, where the bugs become attached. This plant likely inspired those truck stop No-Pest-Strips, which coincidentally, can also consume a hundred insects at a time.

Another carnivorous vegetable, the pitcher plant, attracts insects to a bowl that leads to a trap. Once inside the mouth of the pitcher, the insect finds it difficult to escape. The only bad thing about being a pitcher plant is that it must eat whatever falls in, no matter what. The last time something like that happened to me I was in my high school cafeteria.

Hooded pitcher plants have an additional angle. Over the throat of the plant that catches the insect hangs a hood. Any bug that tries to escape hits the ceiling and falls back in. It's a lot like being the Tidy Bowl Man with the lid down.

The huntsman horn is the tallest pitcher plant. It is large and open-mouthed, which reminds me of some people I know.

Two other groups of carnivorous plants are the bladderworts and butterworts, species apparently named by a scientist in a really bad mood, maybe from something *he* ate.

The bladderwort, an aquatic plant, feeds on crustaceans, worms, fish, and such. When the critter touches the bladder, the lid opens

9

and water rushes in, sweeping the visitor with it, just like flushing a toilet.

The butterwort, on the other hand, uses the strong adhesive on its leaves to trap insects. When lunch lands, the leaf curls around it slowly. It's not in a hurry, primarily because it can take up to a week to digest its food. That's what happens when you don't take the time to chew.

All in all, I never realized how many carnivorous plants there are. It's the sort of thing that makes me very nervous around salad bars.

Weeds . . . I Mean, Wildflowers

"A weed," explained my botany professor, "is merely a plant out of place." I always liked that definition until it struck me that another question was left begging: "Out of place according to whom?"

Evidently, out of place according to us. But what if they're not out of place? What if we're just too close to see the pattern? What if from far above these weeds spell words when they bloom, like G-R-E-A-T, and we're down here with lawnmowers and pesticides taking out the G and R?

It's no wonder we have so many alien sightings. From space, it looks like we've hung out this giant sign that says E-A-T, as if we were the Restaurant at the End of the Universe. And we wonder why whenever someone sights aliens, a cow's missing.

Wildflower gardens are gaining in popularity, because wildflowers are both beautiful and useful. For instance, wildflowers can be used to reclaim barren fields, thereby reducing erosion. The way I look at it is that the weeds will sprout anyway and calling them wildflowers keeps me from having to mow them.

The commercial availability of seeds now makes possible broader applications of wildflowers. One example is the highway department's widespread planting of wildflowers in the median between lanes. You can tell where they've done this by the signs that say, "Experimental Planting. Do Not Mow." I'm trying to find out who their supplier is; I want one of those signs for my yard.

When I look at some of the wildflowers available, like goldenrod, I wonder if their greatest commercial value isn't supporting the market for antihistamines.

11

I have trouble properly identifying wildflowers. I mean, they never look like they do in the book. What I need is a color guide showing various wildflowers as chewed on by passing deer or slept on by a rabbit.

I find some wildflowers especially interesting. Take chicory. This plant has a fleshy rootstock which is used to add a distinct flavor to coffee. If you've ever had chicory coffee, you'll know why people refer to the granules as "grounds."

Other wildflowers have curious stories behind their names. For instance, the dandelion's leaves form jagged teeth that resemble those of a lion. That's how it got its name. I don't think I want to know where they got the name ragwort.

Forget-me-nots are impressive little plants, because they actually defend themselves from insects. The tiny hairs are inclined toward the leaf tip, making it difficult for bugs to climb toward the stem. Why this is important for forget-me-nots, though, slips my mind.

Wildflowers provide food for animals. For instance, the pokeberry is a favorite of songbirds. This becomes evident whenever you hang white laundry on a clothesline. Purple stains abound, as if dropped on a bombing run. I'm not sure whether the birds really like the seeds or just eat them for the sport.

Bloodroot also deserves mention. The bloodroot plant's rhizome, which looks to the layman like a root but is viewed otherwise by scientists, oozes red juice when broken. Luckily, scientists didn't get to name this one. "Blood rhizome" sounds too much like a disease.

Thistles have also been tossed into the grouping of wildflowers. They probably volunteered for this to get away from all those gardeners with the two-pronged thistle-diggers.

Books on wildflowers start with the assumption that you *want* these things to grow in your yard and garden. What I need is a chapter titled, "How To Make Dandelions Common In Your Stuck-Up Neighbor's Yard, The One With The Manicured Look of a Putting Green."

Admittedly, at first I was surprised that other people actually cultivate plants I've always considered weeds. I can see the advantage, though. It would sure make gardening easier.

But gardeners who want to grow wildflowers will generally find them fitting into one of three groups. One is the perennials, which have roots or bulbs that enable them to live for multiple years. Then there are annuals, those that bloom, drop seeds, and die. The third group includes those wildflowers in my yard that get attacked or pulled up weekly and still live forever.

Many gardeners who plant wildflower seeds prefer to do it in the fall. This allows nature to take care of scarification, a process whereby hard-shelled seeds break down. I've heard you can accomplish the same thing in your refrigerator. This is probably true, because I know back in my bachelor days, lots of things grew in my refrigerator.

The texts on wildflower propagation also recommend using pure-strain plants to help preserve the gene pool. This sounds like a good idea. The thought of weeds with hybrid vigor is really scary.

Still, even gardening with wildflowers has its problems. One of the most hilarious discussions I've listened to dealt with weeds in your wildflower garden. I mean, how would you know?

Slugs can also wreak havoc in a wildflower garden by eating your plants. Obviously, this is a problem gardeners need to address, but my guess is that unless you have a *lot* of slugs, there's no reason to hurry.

One reason you may not immediately notice a problem with slugs is that they do most of their eating at night. That's because their wives have them on diets.

Some gardeners recommend putting out saucers of stale beer to attract slugs. It doesn't kill them, but it does make them belch a lot, which in turn makes them easier to locate.

Wildflower gardeners occasionally list winter heaving as a problem, but usually these are the same ones using a lot of stale beer. Just kidding. Winter heaving is the alternating freeze and thaw of the soil, causing the surface to rise and fall back. Then again, that's exactly what happens with too much stale beer.

In any event, there's no question that wildflowers have their place. But I would encourage you to be careful how you plant them. Who knows what you might be spelling?

Critterphobia

Gnuts to Gnats

Anyone who has stepped outdoors, regardless of his pursuit, has encountered gnats. Notice I use the plural here, since there is no such thing as "A gnat." Gnats only come in minimum quantities, COD, with no return address and postage due. They're the bug version of junk mail. No one ever sent off for gnats. If you're starting to get the impression I dislike these winged warts of the woods, you're right.

My first encounter with gnats was on a worm-dunking trip for suckers. Besides fight and availability, these Phyllis Dillers of the fish world don't have a lot going for them and look like they're made from spare parts anyway. They could use help from something other than gnats to glamorize the experience. Sucker streams really need to be infested with butterflies.

We would hunker down in the mud, try to watch our lines for the telltale quiver of a bite, only to have a thundercloud of gnats descend upon us. The insect forecast on sucker fishing trips always reads, "One hundred percent chance of gnats with scattered mosquitoes and sweat bees likely."

Just when I thought gnat infestations could be no worse than on my sucker stream, I grew old enough to go night fishing. At least, that's what I thought the invitation was. With my dad's Southern accent, how was I to know he was saying "gnat fishing"?

If they could ever design a lantern that would attract minnows without drawing in gnats, all those boys at the Coleman plant in Wichita would be running around in four-wheel-drive Rolls Royces.

After hanging our beacon for the buzzing beggars, we were soon fanning, spitting and squinting, while easing our rods up and down to coax crappie. If you can't rub your head and pat your stomach simultaneously, don't try gnat fishing.

Another skill helpful in gnat fishing is the ability to talk with your mouth closed, or at least, through clenched teeth. When the relative gnat index reads 100 percent, any entomologist will tell you that an open mouth quickly equilibrates with the outside atmosphere. In layman's terms, that means your mouth fills with gnats.

Talking through clenched teeth filters out the explorers of the gnat world and looks macho besides. For instance, you can tell by the way he talks that Clint Eastwood has been gnat fishing.

You might think hunters would have less trouble with gnats, since fall and winter months are so much cooler. Admittedly, gnats can't fly with snowshoes on, but since these hardy little headaches have no air traffic control system, they come out under surprisingly adverse conditions.

Turkey hunters, for example, might argue that April should be National Gnat Month. Gnats are the reason mouth calls for turkey hunters are designed to work by exhaling. No gobbler has ever answered the call of a hunter choking on gnats, which sounds something like, "Yelp . . . Yelp . . . Yelp . . . HYECHH-THEUP."

Bird hunters have been known to mistake gnats for distant doves and shoot at them; at least, that was their excuse. My guess, it was retaliation.

Of all the types of hunters, however, gnats are most bothersome for those who pursue groundhogs. When you're glassing a field in ninety-five-degree heat, on your belly, sweating profusely, craving water, trying not to move, a gnat is a torturous beast. Gnats seek shade in such weather—an ear, or a nose will do just fine. Never yawn in the presence of a shade-seeking gnat.

Gnats communicate well with other insects and, in some fields, have been contracted as scouts by yellow jackets. Gnats begin by splitting up; when their prey is spotted, they swarm to block the better escape routes, then herd you to the yellow jackets. If they can get you to belly over a yellow jacket's hole, they get 10 percent commission.

Gnats use natural roadblocks to maneuver hunters away from groundhogs. Besides thistles, there are manure piles. Manure in the August sun can stop a linebacker's blitz, and even groundhog hunters turn to putty once downwind. Gnats move manure piles after dark to create open lanes leading to yellow jacket holes.

Fences are another strategic barrier employed by gnats. Farmers build fences with no consideration of hunters. The strands are too close to get through, too low to get under, and a bit too high to straddle. Gnats no doubt whisper in hunters' ears the farmers' usual reminder, "'Preciate you not climbing over my fences; makes 'em sag." Of course, gnats say it so quickly that only the subconscious can pick it up. To the human ear, it just sounds like a high-pitched whine.

Furthermore, fences around groundhog fields have no gates to walk through. The cows are apparently airlifted in by gnats.

Cattle, intimidated by gnats, cooperate wholeheartedly with their schemes. Should you crawl too far from a yellow jacket's hole and find shade, you will undoubtedly meet someone like #87.

In earlier days, cattlemen kept purebreds, such as Angus or Herefords. Nowadays, they crossbreed for hybrid vigor, and one of the most popular bulls to use is a Brahma, like #87. If you crawl into a Brahma's view, you will personally experience hybrid vigor.

At first, I thought the numbers, displayed on a tag in each animal's ear, were so the cattlemen could keep track. Now, however, I am convinced the numbers are for these hunter-hating bulls to keep track. Last summer, this Brahma was #73.

Obviously, he had a good year.

#87 stays mad. That's because he is constantly pestered by gnats.

Should you see #87 first, ease quickly (i.e. scoot like a rat in a flash flood) toward the nearest fence or tree even if it's directly over a yellow jacket's hole.

If he sees you first, act like a big gnat.

Gnats are repelled by only one known substance. It's not DEET or alcohol; it's old cigars, those crooked, Spanish kind with the matador's widow on the box.

When I was younger and considerably more gullible, my groundhog-hunting associate, Lanny, pointed out the potency of crooked cigars.

"Take one of these and light it, don't inhale, just blow smoke, and no gnat will come within ten feet."

He was right. What he failed to point out, however, were the side effects. First, you can't just exhale on a cigar. Sooner or later you have to inhale and then smoke gets in your lungs. Besides setting off alarms from the Surgeon General, cigar smoke in the August heat causes your head to lift gently off your shoulders until the earth spins, at which point your stomach threatens mutiny.

18

The only recourse is to flip onto your back, preferably not over a yellow jacket's hole, and promise yourself never to touch another cigar if you survive the sudden increase in our planet's orbital spin. If the buzzards don't mistake you for dead and move in to feed, you will eventually recover. But by the time you're able to walk, the cigar will be out and the gnats back in force. Cigars are better avoided unless you can build a little bonfire out of them.

Trudging back to the car one day, having missed a long shot at a groundhog—no doubt deflected by a gnat—for one split second, I glimpsed a small truth in the natural order of the universe. The Good Lord, in His infinite wisdom, gave man something besides groundhog hunting to occupy his mind between the close of spring gobbler season and the opening of dove season, namely, fishing. Bass fishing, that is, not gnat fishing.

I called out in that moment of revelation, seeking the spiritual purpose of gnats . . . all that came back was a chuckle.

Little Bugs, Big Teeth

If you want to get rich quickly, open a dentist's office for insects. Not only are there a lot of them, they all seem to have teeth. The one saving grace is that they each have different habits and attack plans, so at least they don't all bite you in the same place.

Take chiggers, for example. Not much is known about chiggers, at least, not by me.

But knowledgeable scientists say that chiggers are among the least picky of the arachnids, since they are willing to settle for anything from chickens to toads. Even snakes have trouble with chiggers, which raises a couple of questions. How do chiggers find a snake's armpits, or better yet, how do snakes scratch where they itch?

These little specks with teeth have a remarkable ability for locating hosts by sensing the carbon dioxide given off when animals exhale. Which suggests you can easily avoid chiggers in the woods by holding your breath.

Slightly bigger, but still no fun to play with, is the flea. Adult fleas feed on blood and willingly accept dogs, cats, or people, which proves that either fleas are farsighted or your Odor-Eaters need changing.

It has been estimated that a flea can jump distances 150 times its own body length. This is really no big deal. *I* can jump 150 times a flea's body length.

Fleas usually bite in clusters about ankle high, or roughly at a distance above ground level equal to 150 flea-body lengths.

But fleas occasionally fall on hard times, and they've been known to survive up to three months without a meal. This could explain why they have no preference among dogs, cats, or people.

Besides the pain and itch, fleas can also inflict infirmities including heart worm in dogs or the bubonic plague in people. There is no mention of what they do to cats. Maybe fleas figure that with nine lives, cats aren't worth the effort.

Another barely visible pest is the no-see-um. These little nuisances got their name because "that *!?!* hurts like the dickens" wasn't polite to say in front of children.

Actually, no-see-ums are so small they can pass through screen mesh, at least before they fill up on your body fluids.

The reason no-see-ums hurt so much is because of the way they bite. Instead of the syringe-like puncture of mosquitoes, no-see-ums bite with a cutting motion similar to scissors. Insects apparently come with as many options as a Swiss knife.

Should you contribute blood to a no-see-um, you may be interested to know that it was a female. Whichever scientist figured that one out had far better eyes than I do.

Some insects are despised, feared, and loathed beyond just the pain they inflict. Ticks, for example. Think about it, though. But for one bad habit, a tick could be a ladybug.

Once a tick latches on, it can feed until it swells to several times its original size, which would suggest there is still an untapped market for exercise videos.

As if just sucking your blood weren't enough, ticks also carry both Rocky Mountain Spotted Fever and Lyme Disease. The only thing worse would be a vampire with smoker's cough.

Ticks join that group of patient insects that may wait for months, or even years, before their next meal comes. At that rate, they're probably poor customers for dental floss. The reason ticks can live so long between feeding is that their metabolism is extremely slow. In fact, a tick may breathe only a few times an hour, something that works to their benefit since so many have dogs on their breath.

After the female tick feeds, she will fall to the ground and in four to ten days lay thousands of eggs. That is, if the landing doesn't pop her.

When you find a tick, take care to dispose of it properly. This can be done by burning them or dropping them into alcohol. Do not flush ticks down the toilet, since not only can they survive this ordeal, but it really irks them when people do that.

Of all the biting bugs, perhaps the most dangerous are those we classify as bees. More Americans die each year from bee stings than from snakebites, ticks, and rabid animals combined. The only consolation is that more bees also die at the hands of Americans than from snakebites, ticks, and rabid animals.

When around bees, keep in mind that they only sting if disturbed, threatened, or having a bad day.

Entomologists and beekeepers are quick to point out that yellow jackets and wasps are not bees at all. This is about as reassuring and useful as learning that the Doberman on your ankle is not a pit bull.

Yellow jackets, which are actually a type of wasp, have very short tempers. This is because they are attracted to the smells of picnics and then get infuriated at not having been invited.

Honeybees, on the other hand, are true bees and live in colonies containing up to 80,000. That alone is reason enough to *buy* your honey.

Over the years, a number of tips for avoiding stings have been offered, including suggestions such as wearing light-colored clothes, leaving off the strong perfumes, and resisting slapping at bees, which irritates them. Other tips are far less practical. For instance, one author suggests avoiding areas where bees are located, riding with your car windows shut, and leaving nests alone. Since few people engage bees on purpose, this is about as useful as saying, "Don't trip over things you don't see."

Following, however, are a few tips that I've found extremely useful in reducing your chances for a bad bee encounter:

For starters, never impersonate a large flower.

Never substitute honey for suntan lotion.

Always remember, watermelon seeds do not buzz.

Don't ever trick or treat as a bumblebee.

Never, never let anyone convince you that piñatas come in the shape of hornets' nests!

Little Miss Muffet Was Right

Despite their small size, few creatures generate more fear than do spiders. We will send family members out of their way to stomp these eight-legged creepy crawlers, if for no other reason than to avenge the fears of Little Miss Muffet.

And it makes little sense that people should fear spiders. Considering their size relative to ours, what makes more sense is that spiders would fear shoe soles. Imagine the poor spider that wanders accidentally into Imelda Marcos' closet of 5,000 shoes.

Spiders scare us mostly because they surprise us. Who hasn't had these creatures creep into their sleeping bags, sheets, or shorts without notice? Many a lint ball has died a violent death by mistake, committing no crime other than being a dark spot on a light-colored floor.

I have personally had a number of dangerous encounters involving spiders. Usually, however, these were rubber spiders and the incident involved teachers, girls, or humorless roommates.

If you are scared of spiders, you won't be comforted in knowing that scientists have named about 37,000 spider species so far and are not done yet. I'm not sure whether they haven't found them all or just ran out of names.

Some argue that spiders play an important role ecologically, by controlling our insect populations. Still, I prefer Venus' fly traps if for no other reason than that I have never been surprised by one in the dark.

Though most of us hate close encounters with a spider of any kind, oddly enough, we tend to be fascinated with them, especially their webs. I'm not sure whether it's the symmetry, architecture, or the same feeling a bug has before he lands in it.

Perhaps the most fascinating part is that spiders can erect a new web in just an hour or so, less time than it takes me to set up a tent.

Webs used to be a source of amusement for us as kids. We would hunt for the funnel-shaped webs in our shrubs and "tickle" the spider out with a weed. By gently twitching the web at the edge, we were essentially ringing the spider's security alarm. When we tired of that, we would tickle someone's ear with a weed imitating a spider, which essentially led to them wringing our necks.

Sometimes the best way to deal with fear is to understand it. With that in mind, let's take a look at some of those spiders we most fear, starting with the poisonous species.

When it comes to cruelty, few insects can match the black widow spider. She exercises a heartless lifestyle exemplified by mating, then killing her husband. If there were ever a need for marriage counseling . . .

You can easily identify the black widow spider by the telltale hourglass on the underside of her body. You would think her mate would have wised up when he noticed her constantly checking the time.

Reportings of black widows biting humans have declined over the years. This is because black widows prefer dark remote places and, years ago, they commonly inhabited outhouses. Flushing has proven an effective means of control.

The most bizarre story of black widows was recorded in 1899. Scientists at that time were going to great lengths to sort out which spiders were actually poisonous. A group of Russian scientists actually tried to get some black widows to bite them, but without success. Concluding the spiders were nonpoisonous, they brought in a photographer to take pictures of six black widows on one man's chest. As the story goes, a spider panicked, ran down the man's arm and bit him. Scientists have since concluded that there is an inherent danger in being photographed.

Another poisonous spider, the brown recluse, has on its back markings in the shape of a violin. Presumably, this indicates that you shouldn't fiddle with it.

Some spiders just look horrible. The best example is the tarantula, which combines both size and hairiness to scare those prone to arachniphobia. These spiders look like a granddaddy long legs on steroids.

Another disgusting specimen is the spitting spider. This one spews a venom-laced strand of glue at its victims, whose last words are something that translates into, "Oh, Yuck!"

One spider I find interesting is the cobweb spider. I've often wondered if these bugs have a complex. Imagine spending your entire life with a genetic imprint that makes you go stand in the corner.

The young of cobweb spiders leave home by drifting off on a wisp of web in search of other corners, or for the less fortunate, the nozzle of a Hoover.

A group of spiders that sounds unique is the crab spiders. Over one hundred species of crab spiders live in the United States and, as a group, depend on concealment for both safety and for attacking unsuspecting prey. They have the unusual habit of imitating an odd assortment of objects, including bird dung. This may also explain what makes them so crabby.

I find one spider beneficial—the large yellow and black argiope that builds webs in my tomatoes. Not only does it eat the insects, but as big as that spider gets, I suspect it also scares away the rabbits.

But the only spider I can honestly claim to like is the granddaddy long legs. I'm not sure if it's that they don't look intimidating or if I've just been taught to respect my elders.

In conclusion, if your fear of spiders has still not diminished, consider this. According to statistics, bees and wasps cause far more deaths than do spiders. I'm sure statisticians come up with numbers like this to eliminate our fear of spiders. Only it didn't work for me. Now I'm also scared of bees.

Crawling Skin, Yours and Theirs

Mention snakes around a late-night campfire, and you'll generate enough sweat to drown the flames. Even people who never encounter snakes fear them. This reputation is undeserved. To put it in perspective, few among us fear cars, yet many more people are killed by cars than by snakes. Of course, some of this fear of snakes is justified. For instance, one difference is that after a snakebite, you can't get towed in.

Spawned by fear, many ridiculous myths have evolved. My favorite is the fictional account of the hoop snake, a reptile that supposedly bites its own tail and rolls downhill to get away. Anyone who knows snakes realizes this wouldn't work, because at the first bump the snake would swallow itself and disappear.

The best way to allay fears is to better understand our friend the snake.

To start, let's look at the animal's features. Snakes have no ears. This works out to the rattlesnake's benefit especially; otherwise that constant racket would drive him nuts.

Likewise, snakes have no eyelids, explaining why they become so agitated during games of "Made You Blink."

Some observers argue you can tell the poisonous snakes from the nonpoisonous by their eyes. Poisonous snakes usually have elliptical eyes, and nonpoisonous snakes have round eyes, except for one pesky little species that thinks it's humorous to squint.

Poisonous snakes generally deliver their venom using fangs, which may be in the front or rear of their mouths, depending upon whether they ever wore braces.

Many people ask me how a snake can feed on prey larger than itself. Two special features allow this. One is a hinged jaw, which lets it open its mouth wide. The second is an elastic skin, which was used in the Colonial days to make stretch pants.

Many snakes feed on prey they swallow whole, sort of the way my college roommates used to eat. These snakes typically feed about once a week, especially the bachelors.

A snake constantly flicks its tongue, a habit employed for two reasons. First, the reptile's scent organ, called the Organ of Jacobson after an early explorer now missing, is used to perceive smell. The constant flicking delivers scent particles to this organ. Another reason for snakes flicking their tongues is that in hot, dry areas they have a lot of trouble with chapped lips.

Snakes move around, but only for specific reasons. For instance, they might be hunting, seeking favorable temperatures, or searching for a place with additional closet space.

Their slithering mode of travel is best described as a side-to-side motion based on their bodies' contact with the ground. In fact, snakes on slick surfaces can hardly move, something useful to remember if you're ever chased by snakes near a glacier, plate glass window, or across the floor of a fast-food restaurant.

Snakes do not migrate during the winter, instead spending the season holed up in a suspended state. Besides, should a flock of snakes fly into Florida, it would scare the body fluids out of most tourists.

Two or three times a year, snakes shed their skins, a process whereby they literally crawl out, leaving behind one intact shell. Immature snakes shed more often, especially if their friends are doing it.

Courtship and mating among snakes can be a complex affair, beginning by establishing for sure which end is the head. Following breeding, snakes commonly disperse suddenly and, afterward, rarely call or send flowers.

A number of snakes have notable characteristics. For example, the rattlesnake's habit of vibrating its tail is a sign of fear, which, I hate to admit, I also exhibit.

The family of snakes known as pit vipers excel at sensing temperature changes. This helps them to locate warm-blooded prey and to crash barbecues.

The spitting viper has the nasty habit of spitting its venom up to a distance of eight feet, something it picked up by watching old westerns.

Perhaps the best known and most feared snake is the cobra. Seeing this snake rise out of a basket to the tune of a flute practically broke me of doing laundry.

Actually, the rather obscure sea snake is far more poisonous, a fact that, according to some historians, explains why surfers originally decided to stand up.

Pythons are among the largest snakes and have been known to eat large mammals such as goats, leopards, and sheep. The rumor about Volkswagens is totally unfounded.

Another big snake, the boa, has several species, including the rubber boa, sand boa, and feather boa, the latter of which I once saw encircle a large woman. Apparently, many boas are treasured pets, which explains her displeasure when I rescued her.

I should point out that not all people fear snakes. Some capture and handle snakes for sport, a hobby that basically requires nothing more than a general lack of good sense.

I say this because many snake experts report being bitten several times over the course of handling thousands of snakes. This raises the obvious question, namely, "Where were these people's mommas?"

Finally, snakes even provide commercial benefits. For example, the most specialized handlers can find work extracting venom from poisonous snakes, a process referred to as milking. I have not personally witnessed this, but suspect they use very short stools.

Nonsense for Naturalists

SHELBY

Night of the Possum

Rain pelted the roof in a steady drumroll, the kind that drowns out all sounds except those that insist on being heard. With woodlots and peach orchards surrounding the house, lights far away struggled to penetrate the gloom. It was a night for sleeping, for warming by the fireplace. The smell of fresh coffee drifted in from the kitchen as I listened to the patter and stared mesmerized into a window that offered nothing back but my own reflection.

Over the sound of gutters gulping rain came a howl that pierced the walls like the wail of the Hound of the Baskervilles. A single howl. Had I imagined it? Then another. And it came from my dog pen.

Reluctantly, I pulled on my duck hunting coat and paused. Was it the possibility of some danger without, or merely a dread of the storm that made me hesitate?

Whether she wanted to help or feared staying alone I didn't ask, but my wife, Jan, grabbed her raincoat and followed me out. By the time we reached the dog lot, the floodlights from the house had lost their strength, absorbed in bits by the rain. The long, broad run of wire, designed to give hunting dogs some room, lay ahead like a trap.

My dogs continued wailing. Then in the darkness, I heard it—a hiss, carrying through the black gloom, like the breathing of Darth Vader in some *Star Wars* rerun. The hood of my jacket fell forward cowl-like as I clicked on my spotlight, throwing its beam into the pen.

The hideous face that caught the light snarled menacingly. Despite my size advantage and a pair of hounds driven into a frenzy, the runty intruder showed his sharp teeth in a wicked smile devoid of fear. A possum in a dog pen is truly a terrible thing.

"Go get 'em, Obi-Wan Kenobi," Jan snickered through the rain. A quick assessment revealed that the little beast had probably climbed across a limb and down the wrong tree, not a bright act. Of course, no one ever suggested possums were overburdened with brains.

A professor once told me that in the event of world catastrophe, possums were his bet to be the last survivors. "First, they are adaptable. They eat fruit, vegetables, meat, garbage, just about anything. Second, they are too stupid to let even a catastrophe bother them."

One intelligence test I've always wanted to run on possums is to hold two flashlights out at arms' length, one on each side of a possum, to see if it starts to zigzag madly then flattens like a pancake and utters a *bump-bump* sound. It could be their actions in front of headlights are genetic.

After some mental rambling like this, I came back to the possum at hand.

Boy, was he ugly. He looked like an armadillo caught skinny dipping, his shell hung on a nearby bush. He didn't have enough hair to call it fur, and with his pointy little face and naked tail he could pass for an over-inflated rat. Those bared teeth looked like old dentures borrowed from a weasel. But the look in his beady little eyes contradicted his vicious grin, because they shone with all the aggression of a grapefruit.

Perhaps this beast had drifted off to sleep hanging from a slick branch, then lost his grip, disturbed by nightmares of headlights. Or maybe he just ate too many fermented grapes, took the wrong branch home, and started hissing, hiccuping and weaving. In any event, the grump stood nose to nose with my dogs exhibiting some blend of bravery, stupidity, and possibly a hangover.

The next step then was to break up the fight, or should I say, canine/marsupial standoff.

Opening the gate, I first grabbed the Brittany's collar. Legs pumping from enough adrenaline to pole vault, he twisted back to the possum, swinging me around in the mud and flipping my hood down over my eyes. By the time I had recovered, the dog had rooted in like a pig with a mission.

I started again, guiding his forward momentum like a bowler on his final approach to the pins: legs bent, arm extended, striding quickly, to clear the gate.

Jan took the dog and led him to the yard. One down, one to go.

The golden retriever crouched with her head down on the possum's level, matching each hiss with a low growl. The odor of wet dog filled my nostrils like the smell of a week-old gym-class towel. I grabbed her collar with both hands and pulled, but nothing happened. She had turned into seventy pounds of growling concrete. Leaning back to use my weight against hers, I began to slide her through the mud. Each time I gained a new footing, she crept backward, keeping both eyes on the possum as if he were the anchor that held her. Once the golden was out of sight of the enemy, that anchor rope broke and she gave way to my tugs.

I turned the second dog over to Jan as well. She struggled to hold back two dogs taut with contradictory urges—stay and obey or break and attack. Visions of divorce court danced in my head, helping fight down the urge to yell, "Sic 'em!"

Instead, I went back to flush out Darth possum.

He was gone. Not gone from the pen, just gone. Knowing possums are too slow to jump to hyperspace, I searched through the rain, darkness, and expanse of the pen but couldn't see him.

So I trudged back through the downpour, took the smaller of the two possum hounds from Jan, and conducted a mini-hunt in my possum preserve. The Brittany performed admirably, and we were soon onto the elusive omnivore, who had tried to escape detection by moving to another corner of the pen.

I held the straining dog and tried possum-herding toward the gate. Either my shepherding skills were poor or this particular possum needed remedial work in being herded. When I moved up close, he turned to face us, showing his toothy grin and standing his ground. When I backed off, he rested. If he had been one of my sheep, I would have gladly staked him out and mailed engraved invitations to the wolves.

My brain, though dulled by dampness, stumbled upon the thought of a shepherd's staff. Maybe my "stray" possum just needed a push.

Finding a pine limb with a crook like a dog's leg, I reached out and prodded my possum. It rolled over and played dead, or should I say, possum, the one thing at which it was no doubt most adept. That or climbing into dog lots.

This time, the moan came from Jan, not the dogs. Obviously, we were getting nowhere, or certainly, nowhere near the gate.

My temper snapped like the safety on a twelve-gauge Browning pump, something I was tempted to retrieve from the gun rack in the house. Pulling the Brittany, I backed up to think, wondering if a fruity

Ripple or a more expensive Chardonnay would best complement the possum recipes in my *Southeastern Wildlife* cookbook.

That's when he did it. He got up and began to move. Having few thoughts of their own, possums are obviously telepathic. "May the force be with you," I mumbled, and began to concentrate on an image of the beast, apple in mouth, lying on its back in a bed of turnip greens. The possum hissed but moved toward the gate. Concentrating harder, I hissed back, "Roast possum, roast possum!"

As he passed through the gate, the little animal paused, looked back over his shoulder with that snaggled grin and gave a final hiss. But to anyone who speaks possum, it was a beaten sound. Then he faded into the soggy darkness.

With a flair, I threw back my hood and stood triumphant, glaring up into the rain—a true Jedi master. Jan thrust the golden at me. "Here, hot shot. Just be thankful it wasn't a skunk."

The Good, The Bad, and The Pungent

The characteristics of many animals cause them to be loved, feared, or forgotten. Sometimes cartoons or movies will portray animals as angels, so much that we forget their faults. Other times, animals play the role of villain and we forget their virtues. And still other times, common animals live in our back yards, but since they're inconspicuous, we don't remember them at all. Three good examples that illustrate these points live near you, maybe too near.

Just to be fair, let's start with the forgotten one, the flying squirrel. The flying squirrel is a common animal, but one that is rarely seen. Its Latin name is *Glaucomys volans,* which means "gray mouse that flies." Some records suggest that second choice was "mouse that smacks into trees."

Flying squirrels typically inhabit hardwoods, which to them is any tree they smack into.

Besides living in hardwoods, flying squirrels often decide to move into attics. Being nocturnal, they are probably the Civil War ghosts that entertain guests in many bed and breakfasts. In fact, one I visited that was infested with flying squirrels had a sign over the bed that read, "George Washington slept here, but not very well."

One point about flying squirrels deserves clarification. They don't actually fly; they glide. They do this by spreading out the skin extending from front leg to hind leg on each side. When these "wings" collapse, they fold up on each side. The only drawback to this configuration was the squirrels' inability to make armpit noises when they were kids.

The flight itself ends with the squirrel throwing its tail up at landing, either to slow down or because it's unable to scream.

Flying squirrels are mostly vegetarians, gathering fruits, berries, and nuts. A good sign of the self-restraint these animals have is that they rarely drop any of these on bombing runs.

One interesting habit of flying squirrel moms is that they will glide through the air carrying their young by the loose skin on their bellies. This probably explains why the little ones wait until they're three weeks old to open their eyes.

Whereas the flying squirrel keeps a low profile, the chipmunk does just the opposite. In fact, chipmunks must have a really good public relations firm, because in reality, they are little more than upscale rodents, rats in fur coats.

Part of their cuteness comes from all their chirping. Some naturalists feel these sounds signal alarm or attract other chipmunks for mating. Personally, knowing what hams they are, I think they are all auditioning for parts in a Disney film.

Chipmunks store food for the winter and have been known to steal it from each other. I can vouch for this, because I once turned over a hollow stump and found a "Wanted" poster with photos of Chip and Dale.

Despite their lives of crime, chipmunks tend to be well liked. They're cuddly, playful, and have never been cast in horror films. But before you think that chipmunks have no concerns, consider that hawks and owls, foxes and coyotes, even dogs and cats prey on chipmunks. There are more animals eating chipmunks than athletes eating Wheaties.

Chipmunks have the charming habit of overstuffing their cheeks with seeds, as do hamsters. I'm not sure whether this is for transporting the food or if it's just to make them too wide for most other animals to eat.

Chipmunks can also climb, my brother and I learned at an early age. One day our cat cornered a chipmunk in a boot on the porch. We rescued the poor fur ball, put him in a makeshift cage, then took him indoors. Kids typically aren't good cage builders, and chipmunks know this. Ours bailed out and promptly ascended the kitchen curtains to determine the proper route for departure. As it happened, this was the same route my brother and I used before anyone discovered we had loosed a chipmunk in the kitchen.

Another wild creature we kept for a short while was a skunk. Let's get right to the point on this one. Skunks stink. Scientists confirmed this when they tagged the skunk with its genus and species, *Mephitis mephitis.* Since the Latin word mephitis means "noxious gas," the skunk's Latin name means something like "twice as bad as you'd ever imagine."

If not for this nauseating means of defense, skunks would be in real trouble. Their eyesight's poor, they can hardly hear or smell, and they can't run fast. On second thought, it's a wonder *I* can't spray that stuff.

Should you encounter a skunk, the proper course of action is to freeze until it goes away or you get sprayed, in which case you should try to overcome the trauma of such a disaster by chasing your friends.

Once sprayed, lots of people have their own concoctions for dealing with skunk odor. Some recommend tomato juice, others lemon juice. But the best solution I've found is a clothespin.

George and Kit Harrison, authors of *Backyard Wildlife,* note that skunk scent has had commercial applications, both now and in years past. For instance, in the 1800s, skunk scent was used to treat asthma. Now it's used to treat visitors who stay too long.

Skunks have also been kept as pets. The one we kept had been found by my grandfather, and a veterinarian had disabled its scent glands. It still acted, however, as if they were highly functional.

We had lots of fun with this skunk. But of all the games we played with it, my favorite was having new people over and surprising them with "Help, Help, There's a Skunk Loose in the House." Usually, they were vigorous participants until they learned it was our own skunk, and that he wasn't loaded.

Skunks come into the world in litters of five or six, deaf, blind, and holding their noses. When baby skunks begin to go out with their mother, they follow her in single file. Most early skunk fights are over who has to bring up the rear, since they are all aimed that direction and you never know when one of the youngsters might hit a bump and misfire.

Skunks are omnivorous, meaning they eat plants or animals. This makes sense if you think about it. I mean, what could smell bad to a skunk?

Still, as with most other animals, skunks do have their own predator: the owl. Either these birds can't smell, or else they mistake skunks for cats in the dark.

In retrospect, it's odd the way we categorize animals. The good aren't always so good, and the bad aren't always so bad. But you can bet the pungent will always be pungent. Unless you're at my house, and then he might not be loaded.

Of Flycatchers
and Goatsuckers

I grew up in a small town, so I was twenty before I met anyone who considered watching birds a sport, unless you count the St. Louis Cardinals or Baltimore Orioles.

About then, I made friends with a serious birder, but one who had not spent much time around hunters or practical jokers, much less both in one. The first time we went out together, whenever he spotted a bird and said, "Look there," I replied with, "Now wouldn't he be pretty on a bed of rice."

It only got worse when I pointed to a bird and he asked, "Range?" and I responded, "Or even grilled."

But his introduction made me curious, and since then I have contemplated considerably the sport of birding.

Admittedly, when I began I knew little about birds. For instance, I thought a flycatcher was one of those sticky strips that hangs by the door in a truckstop diner. Ernie Ford was the only Tennessee warbler I was aware of, and I figured dark-eyed juncos must lurk in back alleys.

Since then, I have discovered that a bird's name can help you learn its habits or characteristics. But still, exceptions occur. Otherwise, the red-necked grebe would be spotted primarily at honky-tonks and tractor pulls.

Bird names provide ample fodder for pondering. For instance, a whip-poor-will is actually a goatsucker. Now there's one to start a bird brawl.

As I delved into bird names and classifications, however, I found the knowledge somehow comforting. For instance, I was pleased to learn there really is something called a snipe. Now I don't feel so bad about sitting out there all those afternoons holding that sack. I just wish I could have caught one.

Yet I wonder if naturalists weren't getting even when they named some birds. Take the catbird. Whoever named that one must have been awakened early and placed that moniker as a curse.

Bird names have crept into our daily vocabularies. Dozens of times my friends and family have seen traits in me that reminded them of these noble and elegant creatures, prompting remarks such as:

"Mize, you dodo! You're crazy as a loon."

It's no wonder I take to birding.

One of the goals of birding is to identify the bird at hand, or the two in the bush, but before you can identify a bird, you must see it.

Seeing birds would be easier if most of them weren't so well camouflaged. It's as if all of them bought feathered jumpsuits from L. L. Bird.

One observation I made as I flipped through the bird book: the males are generally brightly colored and the females are camouflaged, which says something about their intelligence. If you had to guess, which do you think has heard of cats?

Birds would also be easier to spot if they didn't flit around so much. On one birding trip in a wetland, I saw a *bunch* of little birds constantly flitting to and fro. Of course, considering my eyesight, those could have been mosquitoes.

Spotting birds, however, is a skill you can learn. One expert birder told me, "When I look into a thicket, my mind filters out everything that's not a bird."

The first time I tried that, I fell into a hole. Now, I set my mind filters to include birds *and* holes.

Another technique for seeing birds is identifying the places birds are likely to inhabit, then looking for them there. As a last resort, you could create such a spot, with bait, cleared ground, or an inflatable bird bath.

Practically every birder finds binoculars a necessary aid. But beginners can be intimidated by technical terminology when they shop for their first pair. Let me give you a few pointers, beginning with the rating system. Consider, for example, a pair rated 7 x 35.

Just remember that the first number describes the magnification and the second number is an indicator of brightness. To find the relative brightness, simply divide the first number into the second number and compare values among different binoculars. The higher the number, the brighter the view.

Furthermore, multiplying these two numbers gives a fair estimate of their price. After studying these factors and my budget, I settled on a pair of 2 x 6's. I can't see much, but what do you expect for twelve bucks?

Once the bird is spotted, though, you still have to identify it. Unfortunately, this isn't easy either. Often, the bird is partly hidden.

In such an instance, experts recommend looking specifically for features that help in identification, rather than trying to see the entire bird. For instance, if a large bird goes over carrying a baby, you don't have to see the whole bird to know it's a stork.

Many field guides are available to help you sort through the myriad of options. The most helpful, of course, is the kind that has feet and carries binoculars.

Part of my problem is that I have yet to find a book laid out in a manner useful to me in the field. They're usually so complex no bird will sit still long enough for me to find its picture. I need a guide with a whole chapter titled, "Birds That Were Gone By The Time You Looked Them Up."

I've noticed that expert birdwatchers can instantly identify birds, even at a distance. I suspect there's an unwritten code among birders that in the presence of a novice, everyone agrees on the first name blurted out. I mean, how would a beginner know the difference?

Among the features that supposedly help in identification, the one I least understand is posture. I have a hard time distinguishing between a rufous-sided towhee that slumps and an American robin with a bad back.

A characteristic I *have* found useful in identification, though, is the bird's pattern of flight. For instance, erratic flight indicates it's either a woodpecker or a bird that's eaten too many fermented grapes.

Furthermore, if the bird regularly runs into tree trunks, you can bet it was the fermented grapes.

Migrating birds, say the experts, offer the greatest challenge in identification. For us Southerners, Northern birds would supposedly be the toughest. I wonder if it's because of their accents?

Getting close to a bird helps you see its more subtle features, particularly if you have not scared it. To do this, many birders construct blinds.

My first attempt was too successful. I couldn't even see *out*. Some disoriented beaver thought I was in his lodge.

Birders have also been known to use calls to attract birds into the open. I haven't mastered this yet; my squeaker still sounds too much like a cat.

Of course, you can also buy records of bird calls, either to learn their voices or to attract them. If nothing else, I have found that at higher volumes, these records are great for waking the kids for school.

Perhaps one of the aspects of this sport that makes it popular is that it can be brought into your own back yard. For instance, hummingbird feeders can get so covered up with hummers that the little rascals have to go into holding patterns to wait their turns. On a good day, your porch will be busier than the Atlanta airport during Christmas vacation.

Some people establish elaborate feeding stations in their yards. With the quantities of seeds these birds consume, it's a wonder they can still take off.

Bird houses attract birds as well. We put up several in our back yard and, as an added incentive, offered a frequent visitor program. After three successful nestings, I'll ship them all south by UPS.

For a little variety, I have been trying to attract birds of prey. Besides being fascinating to watch, there's nothing like a circling red-tailed hawk or peregrine falcon to keep the neighborhood kids out of my yard.

Looking back on my years of birding, my most memorable sightings came while I was doing something other than birding. For example, on one duck hunt, an owl buzzed my decoys. Another time, on a fishing trip, I saw a hawk catch a snake and fly away with it dangling.

Probably that's why birding is so popular. How many other sports can you claim to be participating in while you're doing a lousy job at something else?

Bats in Your Belfry

Bats fascinate some people and instill fear in others. For the most part, few animals are so misunderstood yet so beneficial. And the natural history of bats bulges with interesting trivia. For instance, you may not know that bats are the only flying mammal, quite a blessing when you consider that cows and whales are also mammals.

In addition, bat species number over 950, divided into two groups: those that feed on fruit and those that feed on insects. This could have been the beginning of that age-old argument, "LESS FILLING—TASTES GREAT!"

The insect-eaters provide an important service by holding the insect population in check. Each night, one of these bats will eat as much as half his body weight in bugs, followed by two Alka Seltzers.

To accomplish this incredible feat, bats fly with their mouths open, catching all sorts of insects and hacking at a pitch unheard by humans.

Insects happen to be an ideal meal for bats, because they are high in nutrition and digest slowly, the latter an important feature when you're hanging upside down for hours between meals.

Surprisingly, some species of bats feed on fish. Other bats have been known to swim, which also makes you wonder how often fish feed on them.

The negative perception of bats stems from their reputation as a symbol of evil. Legends describe bats as able to suck the blood right out of people. Perhaps the basis of these legends was the vampire bat, the only known parasitic mammal outside the IRS.

Another widespread belief was that bats were an important ingredient in witches' brew. For instance, in *Macbeth,* Shakespeare referred to the witches mixing "Eye of newt and toe of frog, wool of bat and tongue of dog." Shakespeare never mentioned, however, whether this was served warm or chilled.

Another belief was that bats entangled themselves in women's hair, which in turn would cause a disastrous love affair or death within a year. The old records didn't mention what happened to the woman.

But our society has shown some progress in understanding. For instance, during the 1600s, debtors only came out at night, fearful that daytime exposure would cause them to run into their creditors. These people were nicknamed "bats." Today, we give them Gold Cards.

Even though bats had a bad image, doctors occasionally prescribed them as special remedies. One of my favorites was for people who had trouble staying awake. In the 1500s, it was said that if a person cut off the head of a live bat, tied it inside a black skin, and placed it under his left arm, he would not sleep until it was removed. I would bet money that prescription would still work better than No-Doz.

In the 1700s, North Carolina Indians believed that if a child ate dirt, bats could be used to break the habit. They did this by roasting the bat on a skewer, pulling off the skin, and then feeding the bat to the child. Afterwards, he would never eat dirt again. Certainly, this sounds more effective than a trip to the principal.

Tumors were also believed to be treatable with bat dung, or in one recipe, the heads of seven fat bats. I can just hear the doctor when his prescription failed.

"Are you sure those weren't skinny bats you used? And you're positive there were seven, not six? Well, tell you what, just in case, take two more bats and call me in the morning."

Bats have had commercial uses over the years. Civil War history buffs may know that the South used bat dung to make nitrate for gun powder, which could offer another reason that Northern troops so dreaded the Confederate cannons.

Years later, Dr. C.A.R. Campbell convinced the city of San Antonio to erect municipal bat roosts to attract bats, which would in turn eat malaria-carrying mosquitoes. This would have resulted in heated political debate had the controversy not predated the invention of electronic bug zappers.

Today, bats play an important role in agriculture and forestry by helping birds control the insect populations. You might say bats work third shift.

Some people even consider bats good pets. I would still expect a dog to have its advantages, except maybe for retrieving the evening paper.

To navigate the night skies, bats have developed a skill known as echolocation. Simply stated, they make noises, bouncing sound waves off whatever's ahead. This skill allows them to identify airborne objects, something that must have been unsettling for them in those years following the Wright Brothers.

The discovery of echolocation was no simple task, since it involved watching bats fly in the dark.

Up until the eighteenth century, the bat's ability to navigate in the dark was attributed to sinister powers. Then an Italian scientist named Spallanzani tested owls and bats in half-lit and fully dark rooms, proving that only the bats could navigate in a dark room. How he observed this has never been explained.

Spallanzani then tried covering the bats' heads with hoods and found that they, too, blundered in the dark. Refining this further, he found that covering their eyes had no impact, on his research or his walls.

Reading of his studies, a Swiss zoologist named Jurine covered the bats' ears and found their directions failed. Spallanzani likewise confirmed that bats found their way with their ears. As with many great scientific discoveries, no one believed them.

Not until the 1920s did the bat's navigation system get explained as being related to ultrasonic sound waves and echoes. Either that or witchcraft.

Another area that scientists don't completely understand is the breeding habits of bats. The animals' being nocturnal to begin with makes the situation complex, especially for the parents of teenage bats.

Apparently, the first step in bat breeding begins when the female is awakened by a bite on the neck. Details are sketchy, but it appears that unless the female continues to fake sleep, breeding follows.

Female bats have been reported flying up to 1,000 kilometers to give birth to their young, unless their mothers can come to *their* cave.

Usually, females produce one bat per birth, or rarely, twins. Theories as to why bats do not have litters of six to eight vary, but it could be related to the difficulty pregnant bats would have with takeoffs, landings, and hanging upside down. As you recall, natural selection says nothing about Survival of the Fattest.

Researchers believe that baby bats do not have to be taught to fly. Falling from the roof of a cave and landing on their heads seems to be incentive enough.

Despite the niche bats have carved for themselves, their future tends to be gloomy. Bat numbers are declining, a phenomenon unrelated to their use in medicinal concoctions.

Mostly, the decline is attributed to loss of habitat, particularly roosting sites, and the increased use of pesticides. And what a shame, just when I've learned that having bats in my belfry is a *good* thing.

◉

Greasy Kid Stuff

C. SHELBY

Take a Kid WHERE?!

Like salt and pepper, bread and butter, pigtails and ink wells, kids and fishing fit. Every calendar company in America publishes at least one picturing a sandy-haired kid carrying a cane pole. Calendar producers, however, are mostly grandparents.

Now, don't get me wrong. I like kids. And I think kids should learn to fish at an early age. But like the saying goes, forewarned is forearmed. It's just that most days even four arms are not enough.

Take, for instance, my two kids, Coconut and Gumbo. Picture a five-year-old Swedish female investigative reporter, and that's Coconut. My lower back pains trace back to curling uncomfortably around her little finger.

At the same time, let me say that I guide her through life with a firm hand. But most of the time it's planted firmly against my forehead in disbelief.

Her investigation starts the minute her feet hit the boat floor. Maybe the carpet triggers her curiosity.

"Dad, you know a lot about the outdoors, right?"

As my chest expands, pressing hard against the top button, I answer humbly, "Well, a fair bit."

"Dad, do fish blink?"

I think for a minute. "I dunno. Why?"

"Well, don't they get water in their eyes?"

While I'm sorting through that one, she hits me from the blind side with another.

"Do fish burp?"

"Well, I . . . uh . . . I dunno."

46

"And one other thing. You keep telling me to be quiet 'cause the fish will hear, right?"

"Right." Even as I answer I know she has led with a jab and the hook is close behind.

"Then why don't they have ears?"

The only recourse in such a sparring match is to take the offensive. Otherwise, you'll be quickly belittled, befuddled, and bedeviled, flat on the mat and down for the count.

"Dad, why do fish eat worms?"

"Because they can't get into McDonald's."

"Oh . . . why not?"

"No shirt, no shoes, no service."

The trick to fishing with kids is staying one step ahead of the question and two steps ahead of the boredom.

When Coconut gets bored, she begins practicing her tap dance routines. Lunch is quietly pieced over the side to the ducks. The rubber worms are braided into a headband. I thought for a while that I had the solution to this one as well.

"Coconut, you can take one toy on the boat," I had said.

"OK, how about Barbie's Soda Shop?"

"Sure."

Only in the main channel did I notice the fine print on Barbie's Soda Shop box. "Over 900 pieces," it said, like that was good news. The first time I turned into a headwind, Barbie jumped into the soda-shop phone booth to call the governor for disaster relief funds. Tiny sodas flew everywhere. Chairs tumbled and tables rolled.

No doubt Barbie's designers will soon provide her with her own fishing rig. The box will read, "Included is a miniature tackle box with over 1,200 microscopic crankbaits." Ken will come with his own fly box and 1,376 flies, mostly size 14s and smaller. I can hear it now. "Daddy, can you tie a blood knot in Ken's leader?"

I can barely do that full scale, so I'll recommend that Ken borrow a spinning rod and some of Barbie's crankbaits.

And then there's Gumbo, a three-year-old fireplug. Kids at that age are the inverse of cats. No matter how you drop them they land on their heads. Finesse is learned at four.

Let me describe Gumbo for you.

Have you ever seen one of those Radio Shack robots that bump into walls, bounce off, turn, bump into another wall, beep, buzz, and blow smoke? That's Gumbo in a bass boat.

The happiest person in the family when Gumbo goes fishing is his mother. She stays home.

Gumbo likes to cast and reel. Constantly. Without pause. The fish that catches his hook will be decisive and outgoing, and likes to hang out under boats. Gumbo's cast goes about four feet.

Gumbo likes action. The most effective ploy I've found with Gumbo is to catch a handful of bluegills and let him race them around the livewell. That's good for at least fifteen minutes.

And whatever I do, I never, never, never forget his Snoopy float. In my mind, I've plastered a picture of Charlie Brown wearing a hat and trench coat and holding a Snoopy float, saying, "Snoopy floats—don't leave home without them."

Although fishing with kids sounds just short of impossible, I do have a few tips for you. And believe me, they're based on experience.

First, be sure everyone understands that the capacity of a boat is no more than one kid per adult, regardless of weight. If they overload you, pull the plug.

Second, be sure the kids are spread two rod lengths apart. Otherwise, they get tangled or start sword-fighting with your prized graphites.

Finally, do everything you can to get them into action early. Bluegills, crappies, rock bass, and perch are all good choices and size doesn't matter.

Once, I thought I had finally struck paydirt with Gumbo. As soon as we hit the lake, I saw fish splashing and not a boat in sight. It was a school of white bass. I figured we were in for at least twenty minutes of blinding action.

Steadily, I approached with just the whir of the electric motor disturbing the silence. Still no boats, and still the fish jumped.

Just as I eased up on the school, I heard them: the words that clutch a father's heart, that strike from behind, that close the windpipe as if gripped by the ghost of an ancient arm wrestler, words that conjure fear, remorse, regret, dread.

At the top of his lungs, Gumbo yells, "DADDY, I GOTTA GO TO THE BATHROOM!"

How to Make a Bubba

I have a Bubba. He's seven years old, likes to catch catfish, sleep on the ground, wrestle with puppies, stomp mud puddles, and roll down hills. He'll squash bugs for his mom, feed the dog in the rain, and help Grandpa throw hay to the cows when it snows.

Bubbas are surprisingly easy to make, though it does take a little time. So just in case you'd like to have your own, I'll offer my recipe for making Bubbas. This is an old family concoction passed down through generations.

Start with one small boy. (Obviously, you can achieve a similar result starting with a small girl, but after a few years, she may resent being called Bubba in front of boys. Maybe Bubbette.)

Many people ask about the proper age of the starting product. I would say that you can never start too early, but certainly by the time they are three you can begin mixing in other ingredients.

Add water. The first to add is water. Bubba connoisseurs argue about the best source of this water; my own preference is a pond. You see, pond water is typically infested with bluegills.

Start with small measures. A Bubba-in-the-making often has a short attention span.

Although my Bubba has had multiple water treatments, the one I remember best took place when he was four. It was a small dose, a pond that would fit on a football field. The first throb of spring had sent the bluegills into the shallows, fat bluegills hungry from winter.

We were grubby from digging garden worms. The moist smell of loam still clung to our hands, and the worms had all worked to the bottom of the bucket by the time we reached the pond. I sent Bubba into the bucket digging, and pretty soon a small fist came out with a wriggling earthworm clenched inside.

I threaded it on and tossed it past the creek channel, edging it back. The Snoopy float lay on its side waiting.

Soon enough to prevent a mutiny, Snoopy took off skimming along the surface. I grabbed the line, jerked to set the hook, then let go. Bubba hung on to the rod, and shortly a fat one was flopping in the weeds.

The fish peed a little when I squeezed it to take the hook out—at least, that's what Bubba later told his sister. I filled a second bucket from the pond and stocked our fish. Judging from Bubba's focus, the bucket might as well have been a TV. Bubba stared in like a cat straddling a goldfish bowl.

Back at the house, Bubba studied the spare parts—guts, he called them—while I dug the hole in the garden to bury the remains. Worms out, guts in.

We fried them in butter—the fish, not the guts—and Bubba seemed a little taller at the counter, having fed the family with his four fish, one apiece. Bubba decided he liked water.

Sprinkle with seasonings. As with water sources, Bubba experts debate the best seasonings. Since this is my recipe, I'll pick dove season.

Doves are like bluegills with wings—plentiful, accommodative, entertaining.

If the sun stays low and the gnats fly slow, a small boy will stare into the sky almost as diligently as into a bucket full of fish. Every bird gets pointed and sorted, and those that make the right cuts get fired on. About a third of the time they fold and two-thirds of the time I get asked, "Why'd you miss that one, Daddy?"

When they fall, I send out Bubba.

In between birds, we talk about gun safety, why shells shoot, where the dew goes when the sun rises, and how I know when it's time to quit.

Blend with the hair of a dog. Many an owner has been shaped by his dog. Personally, I like to mix in a puppy. Puppies have their priorities right to suit little boys: sleep, eat, play, sleep. Take a round-bellied pup with oversized feet and mix in a small boy with enough energy to wear out three adults, then blend for one afternoon. Come sundown, they'll both be dog-tired.

Boys can talk to dogs. Not many friends listen so attentively, shifting their heads to stare first with one eye, then the other, occasionally smiling with their red tongues hanging just through their teeth. The dog, not the boy.

Not many friends are ready to go any time the boy is, to any event, in any weather.

Not many friends will play catch, though they can't pitch, will take the blame no matter what's missing, and will stand in when Bubba could have used a two-legged friend but didn't have one.

A pup will eventually lead the boy a little farther out, make him run a little faster, give him somebody to look after when everyone else looks after him.

Chill slightly. By now, you have all the essential ingredients. You just need to chill them and wait. The best way to chill a Bubba is in a tent.

Canvas lost its place to synthetics, but it will never be forgotten. The damp odor filled every breath, sides sagging early in the morning, tightening in the afternoon sun.

When a boy camps, the fences spread so wide that they rarely hedge him in. Sticks, long just an item for carrying and poking, suddenly become food for the fire, disappearing in sparks that pop when logs settle.

Bubba and I went last fall, mostly just to enjoy the chill and the fire. We scratched a snake up out of the leaves and in the night heard birds and bugs that we never saw. Bubba roasted his own hot dog, and I think he ate it.

But it's the fire I remember and the realization in Bubba's eyes that something so pretty could harbor so much danger. With sticks, he teased it, explored it, fed it. And by bedtime, he understood it. Come morning, he wanted to hunt sticks and build another one.

He never complained of hard ground or missed cartoons. His days were filled with exciting non-events around the campground, his head filled with notions such as what it means to help, what it feels like to carry a big stick to throw on the fire, his stick, his contribution.

Bubbas are a lot like chili. With the good ones, you can't really tell which ingredient it was that made it just right, but you can pick up a hint of pond water, smell the hair of the dog, and detect the seasoning of dove feathers, all gelled in a chill night air on a mountain with a view.

Like making chili, it takes time. The better ones are fussed over, coaxed along, encouraged, checked regularly, and watched with just the right amount of interest.

Not chili, Bubbas.

The Princess and the Toad

Boxes of slides begin piling up on my desk during hunting season, growing steadily higher through the holidays. Sorting them seems a terrible chore when there are birds to hunt and dogs to chase. But after the season, just before the fishing peaks, the slides are loaded onto a projector and, like a cup of coffee after a feast, they provide something to enjoy while digesting the experience.

This year's favorites were some hurried shots taken on opening day of dove season. I remember I gritted my teeth as the sun rose, feeling between them the airborne dust that floats over the field on hot dry mornings. Occasionally, we get one of those on opening day, a morning that causes your retriever to froth at the mouth as he glances skyward.

Ten of us surrounded the field this year, not counting my Brittany, Clayton. We covered both ends of the age spectrum, ranging from those hoping for a limit to those for whom it didn't matter. The youngest sat next to me, one hand on Clayton's collar and the other in her pocket. Long blond hair was stuffed into a ball cap, and an oversized camo jacket swallowed the rest of her. Whenever she tipped her head back, eyes wide with anticipation, she looked like an impostor, someone smuggled afield under pretense.

Some might think this had happened, that a dove field is no place for a seven-year-old girl. Seven-year-old daughters, however, disagree.

Were I arguing in a court of law on behalf of such daughters everywhere, I would have years of evidence to support my case.

I could open with one of our early fishing trips to Lake Jocassee. She was three that winter, and both of us were going stir-crazy. So we headed to the lake with a can of worms to fish from the bank.

That was the year of the drought. All our lakes were parched, framed in bare banks where the water had retreated. I picked a sandy point where we could lob our bait out and leave our rods lying there. I figured the little one would ramble more than fish. She did.

Now and then I'd check our bait, and occasionally it would be gone. One of these times, I dug into our can of night crawlers and found none. The toddler was carefully walking around the bank above me, hands cupped.

"Hey," I hollered. "Have you been in the worms?"

"Yes," she called back, matter-of-factly. "I have them."

That's what was in her cupped hands, a writhing ball of tails. She presented them for my inspection and I untangled one.

"What are you doing with them?" I asked.

"Taking them for a walk."

To judge and jury I would ask, who but a natural-born outdoors person would take the bait for a walk?

If additional evidence were needed, I would proceed.

Only about a year later, we connected with some fish on one of those hatches that come once every seventeen years. "Locusts" buzzed that spring, and remembering what happened during the last hatch, I headed for the lake. This time Grandpa joined me and my sidekick.

Locusts hung heavy on the shoreline branches. Stragglers fell occasionally, meeting with the *pop-pop* of anxiously waiting bluegills. We passed these by for bigger game.

Grabbing a limb, I brushed about a dozen locusts into a wire cricket tube and screwed the lid shut. Then I rigged a line with a float, no weight, and a size six hook baited with a locust. As I held the rod and watched the lake ahead, the locust whirled around in circles like a helicopter ride at the carnival.

As expected, my young partner was eye to eye with the locusts in the cricket tube.

Before long, I saw what I was looking for, a V cutting the surface and heading toward the boat, like the wake of a freshwater shark.

I lofted the locust ahead of the V, the float dragging the buzzing insect to the water. Circles of vibrations emanated from the live lure, attracting the searching fish like a homing beam. I passed the rod to the inquisitive youngster, keeping the line in my hand.

The V moved in, an ugly head appeared, sucked in the locust, and moved on. As the line tightened, I jerked to set the hook, then let go. The four-year-old squealed in delight as the three-pound carp took off, zigzagging side to side before eventually rolling over from fatigue.

We repeated this event three more times, each episode highlighted by that little cry of joy, reminding every grown-up within hearing range why we fish. You can fish for food, but you can catch carp for no reason other than pleasure. My daughter's squeal told us that.

Who, I would ask judge and jury, was teaching whom? Who was the expert here?

My next argument on behalf of daughters would consist of an incident that occurred more recently. My daughter and I had joined a YMCA program called Indian Princesses, sort of a father-daughter version of the scouts. Twice a year we would retreat to Camp Greenville for a weekend in the wilds.

Any who returned from that weekend rested could only blame themselves. We hiked, canoed, rode horseback, shot rifles and bows and arrows, and sang around the campfire.

While in the canoe, we had noticed some salamanders. In the corners of the pond, dozens lay in the shallows, offering challenging targets for small hands. Insistently, my bow paddler convinced me to beach and spot salamanders for her.

On the drive home, we talked of tall horses, the crack of rifles, and an archery bulls-eye that shocked everyone but the shooter.

"What was your favorite part?" I asked the Indian Princess, anticipating Old Smoke the fat-bellied horse to head the list.

Without hesitation she shot back, "Catchin' lizards."

Four years later, she was still taking care of the bait.

My closing statement to the court would clinch the argument.

"Go back and read your fairy tales," I would say. "If you look closely, you will notice that the relationship between the Princess and the Toad did not begin with his trip to the castle, but with her trip to the marsh. The reason for this is clear. The Princess fits more readily in the world of the Toad than vice versa.

"As with every good fairy tale, there is a moral. Namely, without a Princess, the Toad would never have become a Prince."

Then I would rest my case.

For you see, I don't know much about cheerleaders, Barbies, or the New Kids on the Block, and what I know about boys kind of scares me. Especially boys whose names appear in the same sentence with my daughter's.

If we find common ground, my daughter and I, it will be the ground beneath our boots. We will both know something about walking night crawlers, fishing with locusts, and catching lizards.

So somewhere down the road, the Princess and the Toad will be sitting in a dove field, and that's where we'll tackle the difficult subjects, such as boys. They do, after all, like to hunt and fish as much as daughters.

Outdoor Hobbies
for *Other* People's Kids

Kids take to the outdoors like terrapins take to a tomato patch, so it makes sense that they would love outdoor hobbies. Parents, the ones who planted the tomatoes the terrapins ate, likewise bear the burden of some outdoor hobbies. Rock collecting and entomology are two you might as well brace yourself for.

Rock collecting starts out innocently. As soon as my son could toddle, we began finding rocks in his pockets. Later he would throw them at his sister, but in the beginning they stayed in his pockets.

In hopes that we could redirect his rock-collecting habits, we bought him a rock polisher for Christmas. Fine print originated on the boxes of rock polishers.

In case you haven't been tortured by one, a rock polisher looks like a miniature cement mixer. You load it with grit, water, and rocks, plug it in, and erosion does the rest. At least that's what the box says on the cover. Inside, the manufacturer elaborates, primarily to keep from being sued. For instance, they claim the rock polisher "accomplishes what it takes nature thousands of years to do." They failed to point out that it also takes about that long with a rock polisher, the only difference being that nature has no electric bill that includes around-the-clock rock polishing.

And this rock polisher sounds like a cement mixer full of rocks. By the time it's done you'll be checking out the Motel Six to see if they really do leave the light on for you.

The whole point of this process, say the instructions, "is to make smooth, round stones just like you find in creeks." Am I missing something here? Why not just go pick up a few from a creek and accomplish in minutes what a rock polisher could do in a thousand years?

The procedure for setting up the rock polisher is something a kid can manage. First, you grab a handful of rocks. Second, you put the rocks in the tiny mixer and cover with water. Then you add the grit.

Now, there are all kinds of grit. You start with coarse grit for the first millennium, followed by medium grit, and you finish with true grit. When you see the price for this stuff, you'll grit your teeth.

The one pitfall in switching grit is disposing of it. You cannot just take the rocks out and dump the old grit down the drain. Remember, you just spent a month making cement. Plumbers buy lottery tickets for jobs like that.

And although this sounds like a lot of trouble for the parents, I'm sure the kids love it. I mean, what kid wouldn't fork over a year's allowance to spend an entire month watching a cement mixer go round and round and round, over and over and over, for the privilege of owning a round rock?

My daughter, on the other hand, has decided that instead of pursuing rock collecting, she'll take up entomology. She spends her spare hours bringing into the house all the things I paid Orkin to keep out.

It's difficult to find a reason why kids shouldn't pursue entomology. After all, a few bugs are not something we're likely to miss. Also, you can begin with little more than a porch light and a jar. Furthermore, it's a lot quieter than rock polishing.

Bug collecting is not a hobby obvious to the general public. When kids hang out on the corner watching traffic, they're hoodlums. When they stoop on a corner under a streetlight, they're entomologists. To the casual observer, the two look the same.

Most kids start with live bugs trapped in a jar with holes punched in the lid. These bugs pass from kid to kid and house to house while mothers fear those dreaded words, "Hey, Mom, I think the lid was loose."

After the novelty of live bugs wears off, or after the bug dies, the kids begin preserving their insects. They do this by inviting them to a Mason jar for happy hour, then skewering their little dried bodies on a pin stuck in a cigar box. If you have a cigar smoker in the house, flipping the lid and finding a bug collection late one night could add twenty years to his life when he gives up smoking—if he survives the first thirty seconds.

As the hobby progresses, your youngsters may want to mount their bugs on the wall for all to enjoy. We did at our house, and after the mishap with the vacuum cleaner, I've discovered why most people cover their bugs with glass.

I've gotten used to seeing rhinoceros beetles, June bugs, and even spiders perched on our living room wall. Except that no matter where I go in the room, their eyes seem to follow me.

I guess with all the opportunities youngsters have these days to get into trouble, I shouldn't complain. Besides, the kids are learning a lot about the outdoors, because that's where we now make them keep the rock polisher and the bug collection.

Camping with Kids

Kids love camping. Making a kid sleep on the cold, hard ground out under the stars is like turning a puppy loose in a shoe factory.

And it's no wonder. Think for a moment about camp food: hot dogs, marshmallows, potato chips—it's all the stuff you won't give them at home.

Kids even like the park rangers. I think it's because they believe Yogi and Boo Boo are hiding nearby.

One of their favorite parts of camping is playing with whatever animal is too slow to get away. Critters you and I find less than huggable, kids will find, hold, and carry around. For example, ever since that weekend campout when my daughter caught the salamanders, she has picked up small creatures and carried them in her hands, pockets, or folds of her shirt. Since then, I've learned an important lesson: before any kid gets in the tent, frisk him.

Perhaps what kids like best about camping is that they have a chance to satisfy their curiosities. Curiosity, however, is a lot like shooting an arrow straight up to see how far it will go. Sooner or later, it comes straight back down. I remember years ago in our old canvas tent that Dad always warned us when it rained, "Don't touch the side of the tent or it will start leaking." I never had the urge to touch the tent sides until he brought it up. But then it gnawed at me like a beaver on a dam-building project. And after everyone seemed to be asleep, one small finger would reach out in the darkness for just one poke.

That's why all modern tents come with a separate rain fly, one that's outside the tent and beyond poking range.

Another thing you will soon discover about kids is that they move at a different pace. Sure, a kid's mile is like an adult's, 5,280 feet. The difference is that a kid's foot is only four inches long.

So when you try activities such as hiking, walking, or scouting with a kid, you will probably later describe them with words such as ramble, stroll, or piddle.

Kids even seem to enjoy camping when everything goes wrong. An adult's disaster is a kid's adventure.

Important lessons in dealing with disasters are absorbed on every trip. Kids learn this mostly by watching their elders. Now there's a scary thought. Sort of makes you thankful for darkness, doesn't it?

One tidbit I learned from my dad years ago was picked up on a particularly soggy trip. The firewood had been rained on until it resembled a sponge more than oak. After struggling with wood chips while the matches dwindled, Dad finally resorted to dumping a cup of gasoline on the logs. The vapors drifted invisibly about ten feet downwind by the time Dad tossed in a match. When the fire caught, flames shot farther than a belch from Pete's Dragon.

The lesson sank in and remains. Oh, I might still jump-start a fire, but now I let my brother light it.

You might think amusing kids in the wild would be a problem; however, that's rarely the case. I've always been amazed that a kid in a room full of toys will complain of nothing to do—yet drop that same two-legged tantrum in a field covered with rocks, and he'll play for hours.

Next Christmas, my kids are getting rocks.

Have you noticed too that kids always focus on little things? Maybe it's because their legs are short and they're closer to them.

But you could stand in front of the Grand Canyon with a kid, and just when you think they're bending to look through the rail fence to take in the view, you realize they're actually just stooping over to watch a bug.

Every mom knows what kids like to play with most in the outdoors. It's the same stuff she finds in the bottom of the washer three days later. Count your blessings that very few wild animals will fit in a kid's pocket and those that will also go out through the drain.

When it comes to exploring around camp, a kid considers himself a modern-day Christopher Columbus, who, by the way, spent most of his time lost.

Perhaps the best part from a parent's viewpoint is that you need very little special gear. Well, maybe just a few things. Normally, I pack one extra bag just for Band-Aids and teddy bears.

Safety, when camping with kids, requires special emphasis. Natural landscapes are filled with sharp objects. I'm a nervous wreck when I see my kids take off like rabbits out of a box trap through jutting rocks and sticks. They seem better suited for a nerf campground.

And kids will flutter around a campfire getting continuously braver. I finally told mine that if they caught fire, Smokey Bear would stomp them out.

Some problems unique to kids will arise. Many kids, for example, are afraid of the dark, something there's plenty of on camping trips. Before you take an outing far from home, you might want to try a practice run in your back yard, just to see if the little tykes try a practice run to your back door.

Also, at night it pays to leave a window or door open on your tent to allow the moisture from your breath to escape. Otherwise, it will condense in puddles and soak everyone. Note, however, that with smaller children, you can leave all the windows open and still have puddles.

Answering nature's call presents a special challenge on primitive camping trips where the only bathroom is behind a bush. Note that kids have no trouble adapting to this; usually adults seem more inhibited. It's just that adults don't *keep* using the bushes after they come home.

If you're thinking of backpacking with a child, consider starting him off with his own pack, even if it's a small one that holds nothing but his lunch. Then, every year, increase the weight gradually. If you plan carefully, by the time he's a teenager, you can have him carrying all the gear.

You might want to continue carrying a small pack, though, so he doesn't catch on, even if it holds nothing more than *your* lunch.

Over the years of camping with youngsters, I've collected a few special tips you might appreciate. For instance, one common suggestion is to establish boundaries around camp. Many experts feel this helps keep kids from wandering off. Actually, I'd suggest you consider a fence.

Also, always pick campsites away from potential danger. Geysers are great, but not under your tent.

Experts also say conditioning is the key to enjoying your outing. Therefore, duplicate the experience as closely as possible before you leave home. I guess this means you eat Beanee Weenees, wake your kids with bird noises, and have everyone sleep with sand in their beds.

In fact, it's a good idea to take along a change of clothes for the last day, even if you're going to a well-populated campground. After having your kids roam the grounds for several days, when it comes time to break camp, you might not want to be recognized.

Finally, explain to the kids beforehand that "Let's break camp" is just an expression. You never know when they might actually be listening.

Go Fish

Fishing for Laughs

I laughed at a fish yesterday.

Normally I don't laugh at fish, but it had been one of those days when I'd had few reasons to laugh. I was a long way from home in meetings with people who wanted what I had but didn't want to give up any of what they had. So when everyone had had enough, two of us skipped dinner and headed for the river.

The river still ran big with the spring snowmelt, and my local fishing partner called it "marginally fishable." The banks smelled of wet muck from the high waters. Gnats flitted drunkenly, as if intoxicated by the humidity.

As soon as we reached river's edge we turned at opposite angles to go apply the river's salve to our wounds. I headed upstream, picking my way through stranded driftwood.

As usual when I am on western rivers, I found myself under-equipped with fly tackle purchased for fishing our small mountain streams back east. My rod was too short, my flies too small, and my leaders too light. Suspecting as much, we'd stopped on the way to pick up a few large, weighted stone fly nymphs and a heavier leader. Secretly, I hoped to hook a fish with enough muscle to snap my fly rod in half, thereby giving me a great tale and an excuse to upgrade.

Otherwise, I'd have to lie about the fish and sacrifice my fly rod to a car door.

Just a hundred yards upstream from where we split up, I noticed one of those spots that softly mutter, "Big fish." Knowing the fading light worked to my advantage, I fished slowly toward it, trying again to get the feel of the nymph on a slack line. The difference between a rock bump and a fish is learned, and I feared I'd forgotten.

I had an hour of light left when I reached the spot that muttered as water rumbled through. Up close it looked better than it did from far away. The river narrowed, forcing all the food it carried through a gauntlet. On each side of the gauntlet, impediments broke the water's force so a big fish could rest in ambush.

Dun-colored moths danced above the water, enticing hundreds of gulls to swoop and feast upon them, gulls white against the darkening sky like an illusion in a planetarium. The world filled with strange sights and sounds like a dream, and the river slowly lulled me into a world of laughing birds and muttering waters.

I began working the nymph from the bottom of the slow water up, from the close side out. Trout face the current in such situations, so starting at the bottom of the pocket kept me from approaching the fish in the direction they looked. With a short rod, I could only loft a weighted nymph so far. Plus, starting close in let me work any nearby fish first, giving each a chance to strike before being spooked by the belly of the fly line over its head.

At the far edge of the pocket lay the gauntlet, and forced through it, the water raced. A trout that fed from this plate must make snap judgments or go hungry, so I shouldn't have been surprised when the strike came like a steel trap snapping shut. But I was. The flush of quail or a hard strike on a line still causes me to flinch.

The line stripped off and the reel handle banged my palm as it spun. Fifty feet of line went into the stream before I could move. Then he turned back to fight.

Many people play fish just to land them. With a big fish, I always have two goals. First, just to get a look, and second, to bring it to hand.

On the way to the river, I'd listened to tales of big fish, browns with gnarled lower jaws and rainbows like torpedoes. My mind was set on big fish when I started and now considered the next step toward landing one. I coached myself to get back some line, but not too much. I needed enough to stretch a little, and I wanted the fish off the bottom to avoid the snags. While fishing the nymph, I'd felt boulders, moss, and snags.

So I walked downstream to meet the fish halfway. If I'd thought about it, I'd probably have given up since no one had met me halfway all day.

But this fish wasn't going to let me think about anything else, and the river had already healed those wounds.

Watching where the line cut the water, I judged the trout's actions below and responded. I pictured us like two old arm wrestlers in a Greek tavern. Since it was my daydream, I got to be Anthony Quinn. Every time my opponent pushed, I held on; every time he weakened, I pushed.

The only difference was that it was like I was arm wrestling in the dark. All I knew was what I could feel. The surges, the pauses, the grunts, the quick breaths all came back through my hand and wrist. I steadily pressed, knowing that fatigue would tip both arms to my side of the table.

Twice more the fish turned downstream, and I walked, keeping loops of line in one hand and the rod high in the other.

The trout teetered on the break of fast and slow water, and instinct may have told him that slower water near the bank would give him a rest.

But I wouldn't let him have it. Lifting to clear him from a sunken log, I brought him up into the shallows. When he rolled onto his side, I slid him ashore.

That was when I laughed.

This fish that I had arm wrestled in the dark was out of his weight class. My mind had been set on five pounds plus, but this trout, though a nice fish, might weigh half that.

He had fooled me. He had wrestled well, used the current where he lacked weight, used his weight when he lacked strength.

The nymph hung sideways in the corner of the rainbow's jaw like a toothpick in the corner of a smile. Having wrestled well, I guess he deserved a laugh, too.

I held him by the tail, which felt like a wiry wrist in my grip, and eased him back into the cold Canadian water. Then I wiggled his tail slowly to resuscitate him, watched him swim away, and wondered how he'd wrestle when he weighed five pounds.

Then I went back to fishing for laughs.

The Purpose of Carp

My high school biology teacher once told me that every species has a purpose. Without a reason to live, a function in the ecosystem, a role in plant and animal society, species disappear.

On warm spring afternoons, this thought alone would get me through classes. Flies? Amoebas? Snails? One by one I thought of a reason for each.

And then there was my favorite, the one that stumped me day after day as the sands of time built a beach on my desk. Carp. What good is a carp? What possible redeeming features do carp possess?

These questions resurfaced recently when a notice from some fish society in Washington showed up in my mail. They were petitioning the government to change the name "carp" to something more acceptable, even marketable. It had worked for other fish, they explained; it would work for carp.

Get serious! My spring ponderings had produced only a herd of shortcomings, centered on the fish's appearance. Before this group can promote carp, even under a pseudonym, they must first solve the fish's image problem.

A carp looks like a rubber toy designed to be stuck on a truck window. Just wet a carp's lips and smack them up against the glass. It should stick, like a Garfield doll with suction paws.

Carp are ugly . . . so ugly they have to spawn in muddy water.

If some kid wants to shock his dad into silliness, just let him slip into the bathroom on New Year's morning and tape a carp's picture to the mirror. Old Dad will hit the wagon so fast it will start rolling.

And the depth of a carp's ugliness would keep a plastic surgeon working for a lifetime. Probably the surgeon would start with the mouth, since carp look like they were designed to feed on grapes. To receive respect, this fish needs something that resembles a jaw, and a few teeth wouldn't hurt.

A bass is considerably more macho, because you can heft it by its lower lip. A carp requires a handle.

An artist would need to be called in next to work on color. Carp are too dark to be described as "sunset gold" and too light for "ancient bronze." They are, quite frankly, "mud brown," a complimentary adjective considering the alternatives.

Another particularly bothersome feature is the carp's scales. These swimming armadillos have plates that look like they were stamped out for combat, not sport. Even catfish look more cultured than carp.

Carp hides wouldn't even make good cowboy boots, being easily edged out by such lovely creatures as ostriches, snakes, and lizards. You could make better boots from possums, hair side out.

Then there's the slime. Grab a carp, and no one will shake your hand for a week. If only we can find a commercial use for the stuff, something like mousse for obnoxious Don Juans, or a college prankster's coating for toilet seats. In a pinch, carp slime could be marketed as a patch for flat tires. But for sport fish, we need something that *feels* better and gives a better grip.

Maybe it's just me, but carp seem to stink. I'm not talking about fishy odor; all fish have that. I'm talking about the fish equivalent of morning breath.

Perhaps it's their diet. Did you ever examine what a carp has eaten? It looks like it camped under a food disposal at a cafeteria. You won't find in their guts shad or other bait fish—you know, carnivorous stuff. Carp appear to live off rotten fruit baskets and kudzu.

The carp's dietary interests don't even present an opportunity for the sporting goods industry. Since they can't sell lures that look like canned corn or doughballs, tackle companies will never promote carp the way they do bass.

While we're calling in specialists to rehabilitate carp, let's get one to train this fish to fight. Carp are methodical, running side to side, side to side. And they never jump. B-O-R-I-N-G. Carp are the couch potatoes of the water world.

You can judge a carp's social status by the openness of its fans. Bass have clubs, trout have clubs, even crappie have clubs. Has anyone ever received an invitation to pay $20 to join Carp Unlimited?

Let's face it, carp are underdogs, the Rodney Dangerfields of the fish world. They are undervalued and unloved. No one ever campaigned for more carp. No one was ever arrested for poaching carp. No one ever made the carp their state fish.

If the guys in Washington want to change the carp's name to something that would make it more popular, I'd suggest they try a variation of "bass."

In spite of my inability to find a purpose for carp, I've remained convinced that my biology teacher must have been right. The fish must have some niche only it can fill in the scheme of life. After all, it continues to thrive in almost all fresh water. Time and concentration have suggested a single redeeming feature, the only one I've been able to come up with: Carp are an uplifting species to ponder, because no matter how bad you have it, you're probably in better shape than a carp.

Crappie Confusion

The longer I'm around crappie fishermen, the less I understand them. For instance, crappie fishermen will spend all morning looking for the thickest underwater brushpile in the lake, then spend all afternoon cussing about getting hung. They will plunk down hundreds of dollars on high tech equipment, then fish with cane poles. And the first thing they do with their new boats is squeeze them through flooded timber, grass or logjams, banging the bottom, clogging the prop, and scraping up the sides.

Perhaps crappie fishermen act this way because crappie fishing itself can be confusing, if not contradictory.

The doctrine on locating crappie, for example, says to find structure so thick that the only way to flush them out is by outfitting a beagle with a snorkel. Ask any tackle shop owner or marina operator and he will confirm this basic truth. But did it ever occur to you that these guys sell jigs and hooks for a living? What if all these years the crappie were lying on smooth bottoms, but all tackle dealers were steering you into timber? Makes you wonder, doesn't it?

Lots of fishermen will submerge Christmas trees to create an impenetrable crappie heaven, again at their tackle dealers' recommendations, if their lake's cover is sparse. A Christmas tree, by the way, is probably the thickest bush on the planet and the one most likely to grab your hook. But let me ask you, what's so special about Christmas trees? Why not Easter baskets? They would certainly be easier to fish, and crappie are more likely to bite around Easter than Christmas anyway.

My problem with Christmas trees is that once they are submerged, I can't find them. Next year, I'm leaving the lights on.

Crappie fishermen have many methods of locating these fish, including drifting, trolling, and even casting into likely spots along the bank.

A cane-pole fisherman I know once tried tying monofilament to a divining rod that was tuned for crappie. He never could get used to it. Every time the tip dived to point at a fish, he thought it was a bite and yanked his bait away before the crappie could get it.

During the spawn, some fishermen even say they can find crappie by smelling them. As for me, I've always preferred fishing for something a bit fresher. Besides, I don't believe anyone can smell a fish that is under five feet of water. More than likely, these guys are catching a whiff of other fishermen getting skunked.

But there's no doubt that crappie are most aggressive during the spawn. On a good day, you can't tell if your bait's being eaten or mugged.

Conversely, the most difficult time to catch crappie is in the dead of winter. That's because in frigid weather, crappie go into deep holes and slow their metabolic rates, much like a bear. Only difference is, nobody jigs for grizzlies.

Kids make great crappie fishermen. Crappie seem to know when there's a kid holding the rod. I don't know whether it's the vibrations in the line, the constant noise, or the Snoopy float.

During the summer, daytime action for crappie slows down, so lots of crappie anglers turn to night fishing. My dad got me into this as soon as I turned thirteen, noting it was one of the few things a teenage boy could do after dark that was neither immoral nor illegal.

One thing that has always confused me, though, is why night fishermen tie up to bridges. For many years, I did likewise thinking that crappie must like bridges. More recently, however, I have come to the conclusion that fishermen just hate anchors.

Some people wonder how to get crappie to bite at night. Here's a little trick I've found that works every time. Lay your rod down, hold a cup of scalding coffee in one hand and a floppy sandwich in the other, and, if possible, try to balance the open thermos on one leg. Then just wait. This technique is so effective that bait is optional.

Crappie fishing has been on an upswing in recent years and tackle manufacturers have taken note. Boat manufacturers have even begun to develop models especially for crappie fishermen. But what is a crappie boat supposed to do, stop at every stump? Or run into it?

I wonder, however, if many companies aren't making tackle more complicated, and therefore more confusing, than it needs to be.

71

Take the cane pole, the essence of simplicity. Today, if you try to buy one, it's either telescopic, telesonic, or freeze-dried.

And reels—the claims they make are hard to believe. One manufacturer offers a reel designed to put your line exactly to the depth where the crappie are located, every time, guaranteed. I just have one question. If I don't know what depth that is, how does the reel know?

Lure manufacturers are on the same trend. Take jigs, for instance. Now they come in a 1/100 ounce size. It would make more sense just to bait a hook with lint.

And plastic baits are much the same. Now you can buy one that looks like a minnow, wiggles like a minnow, and smells like a minnow. Why not just buy a minnow?

If manufacturers really want to help me out, they should invent a hook that knows when to let go. Then I'll fish any brushpile the tackle dealers want to put me on.

With the growing interest in crappie fishing, it was only a matter of time before tournaments sprang up. A few guys are even beginning to make a living on the tournament trail. If I ever made a living on the trail, it would be because I was paid to follow pack mules with a shovel.

The reason I can't make it as a tournament fisherman is because other fishermen always catch larger crappie than I do. I keep hearing them talk about slabs. If I were really honest, I'd have to call mine slivers.

Besides, I don't have the right frame of mind for tournament fishing, and I suspect others are similarly dispositioned. They're already too competitive. For instance, I once fished with a guy who notched his cane pole every time he beat me fishing. It got so bad it looked like he was carving a flute.

Despite all this, if I were redesigning crappie, I would really only address two faults. First, it takes a long time to clean a mess of them. Of course, the way I clean fish, I can make a mess with just two.

But cleaning them is well worth the trouble because crappie are one of the best-tasting fish in the country. Whenever I sit down at the table, I give thanks for being at the top of the food chain. In fact, when fried crappie are on the table, you might think my food chain was hooked to a winch.

The second problem with crappie is that they have soft mouths. As a result, you will never see one chosen as mascot for a dental association. The reason is clear: no teeth and weak gums. Of course, they might make a great market for dentures.

Tinkering with nature, however, may not be the answer.

I knew we were in trouble when I heard about a fisheries biologist trying to breed a crappie with a tougher mouth. On the surface, it sounds like a good idea. I lose most of my crappie because of their soft mouths. The only problem is, the biologist was trying to correct this shortcoming by crossbreeding crappie with a fish notorious for a tough jaw, which just happens to be a piranha.

Assuming things go as planned, he might end up with a fish having a tough jaw. On the other hand, he could also end up with a panfish that gums you to death.

Of course, even this may not be all bad. It would definitely cut down on water-skiers.

Admittedly, crappie fishing can be confusing. Maybe we would all be better off, however, to just accept crappie as they are and spend our time figuring out how to keep from getting hung.

Catching Night Crawlers by Helicopter

Obtaining a small business loan during tough economic times is somewhat like trying to potty-train a toddler, difficult and messy. It's even worse when the money is for purchase of a helicopter to be used in a large-scale bait-procurement operation. In such a case as this, the toddler might as well be wearing Gucci diapers.

But that's precisely what led Gill Yates into the Second National Bank of Floyd that fine April morning when he should have been pumping gas down at the Chevron station.

Yates strolled through the double front doors and stopped, waiting for his eyes to adjust to the reduction in light. The swinging door unfortunately hadn't swung yet and came around sharply, popping Gill on the backside and ushering him unceremoniously into the lobby. He was still smarting when Dollar Bill Culligan addressed him from a side office.

"Yates, did those doors get you again? Well, git in here and sit if you can, I want to keep an eye on you. This bank can't afford a lawsuit or higher insurance premiums and you're an accident waiting to happen. Now, what's this about you wanting a loan?"

Dollar Bill didn't mind his nickname, plastered on him by fellow alumni the day he accepted the job of loan officer at the Second National Bank of Floyd upon his graduation. His relationship with Gill went back to the second grade, when he assumed the responsibility of keeping Gill awake in Mrs. Greensworth's class. Mostly, Dollar Bill had been unsuccessful in this responsibility, but he did manage to prod Yates from one grade to another, ceasing with a solid thump during the graduation ceremony.

Now Yates was here to borrow money, and Dollar Bill sincerely hoped Yates would stay awake during this initial interview. "I need money for a helicopter," explained Yates. "I want to start my own business."

"Well, let me get out my loan application forms so I can take a few notes. What are you going to do? Haul cargo, passengers, emergency medical patients?"

"Not exactly. I'm going to catch night crawlers."

Dollar Bill peered over his glasses. Laying down his pen, he leaned back in his chair and folded his arms. "Maybe you'd better fill in a few details on this harebrained scheme."

"It's not so harebrained," said Yates, looking sadder than a puppy when his playmates are sold. "Did you know that the Chevron can't keep night crawlers since the new lake was built over by the Parkway? We have to pay a dollar a dozen when we can get them. I think I can catch large quantities cheap enough to make money at ninety cents a dozen."

"With a helicopter?"

"That's just for spotting them. What I plan to do is lease worm rights in all the pastures around Floyd. I'll use the helicopter to fly over these fields and locate concentrations of night crawlers using an infrared scope. Then, I'll call in the troops by radio."

"Troops?"

"Boy scouts. Troop Number 68 has offered to work four nights a week at minimum wage. When I call, they'll be dispatched right into the fields with flashlights and buckets and catch the slimy little jokers. I'll come back around in my pickup, collect the buckets, box the worms, and sell them to the Chevron."

"For ninety cents a dozen."

"Right."

Dollar Bill put his face in his hands. Speaking through his fingers, the interrogation continued.

"Gill, can you fly a helicopter?"

"Well, no. But I'd figured on learning."

"I see. Are those boy scouts prepared to . . . no, let me rephrase that . . . do they have experience catching night crawlers?"

"I'd have to teach them, but I'm about the best worm grabber in these parts."

"I see. Do you have any idea how many night crawlers you would have to catch to justify a helicopter?"

"Oh, about a thousand dozen a week. Maybe eight hundred if I can get my costs down."

"That's a bunch of worms. The Chevron sell that many?"

"Me and Arnie go through at least a hundred cans just on Saturdays, and we always run out. If I had to, I could probably run a worm route to four or five other bait shops."

"And you can't do this without a helicopter?"

"Dollar Bill, you know as well as I do that you can't tell what's on a worm's mind. Some days he'll be on high ground, some days he'll be in the bottoms. With a chopper, I could find out quick and call out the troops. Dollar Bill, this is a gold mine. You should be able to see that."

"Like your frog farm? And your grub ranch?"

"Those were different. How was I supposed to know the frogs would eat all the grubs and then hop off ungrateful?"

"Yes, you never can tell what's on the mind of a frog."

"Or a grub," added Yates.

"Gill, this one is too big a loan for me to decide on. It has to go to the district office. Are you honestly going to make me send in your night crawler scheme for approval?"

"Dollar Bill, two years from now, you'll wished you owned stock."

"One last question, Gill. Where did you get the idea for this scheme?"

"From Mrs. Greenworth's second-grade class."

"But you always slept through that."

"Well, it was one of those days you nudged me. During story time, she was telling one of her tales, I don't remember which one . . . I was still groggy from waking up . . . but she said it plain as day."

"Said what?"

"She said, 'And remember, class, the whirlybird gets the worm.'"

"Gill?"

"Yeah?"

"I wish I'd just let you sleep."

Bait on a Budget

Fishing costs money and, depending on how you approach it, possibly lots. After you buy a boat, an electronic fish finder, several rods and reels, and all the licenses that are required, your checkbook will be squeezed thinner than a sumo wrestler's bungee cord.

Luckily, economizing is possible when it comes to bait. A number of items can be dug, trapped, or purchased cheaply.

Let's start with some you can catch yourself—night crawlers, for example. During the summer, these slimy wigglers ease above ground on damp nights just to taunt roosting birds. To catch a bucket full, you start by locating a field where they abide. Then, you sneak along with a flashlight and bucket until you see one. If he is very long, has diamond-shaped markings, oval eyes, and fangs, keep looking. When you finally spot a night crawler, quickly grab him before he can get back in his hole.

A second method of catching worms involves inserting two metal rods into wet ground and connecting them to an electrical charge. This thrill drives the worms to the surface to do the Dance of a Thousand Volts. This technique has fallen into disfavor, however, since standing on wet ground while you do this will also cause you to do the Dance of a Thousand Volts.

Crickets, likewise, are easy critters to catch. Simply dampen a newspaper, lay it on the ground, and weight it down with rocks. In a day or two, crickets will have moved in under it, unless you used a classified page with ads for bird feeders or pesticides.

One bait that fish love is the grub worm. These delicacies live in rotted logs and under mulch. For some reason, however, I rarely find more than one. I may not catch a big mess of fish, but I usually don't exceed the limit either.

Sometimes, a bit more daring is required, such as when you fish with wasp larvae. Not only do you have to fight off the parents to get the nest, but you have to use the larvae before they hatch. Still, wasp larvae come in a handy carrying case—the nest—and bluegill love them, so they are worth the risk. I'd just be sure not to carry them in an inside pocket.

Locusts drive fish into a frenzy whenever they hatch. Unfortunately, this tip is only applicable once every seventeen years.

Some baits you can collect offer false savings. Minnows, for example, can be seined or trapped, so the initial supply is free. But you can no longer just haul minnows in a bucket. Nor is the livewell on your boat acceptable, since it is square and minnows need a round home. So some boys who now drive BMWs designed the Baitwell, a round, aerated tank that costs just pennies less than a lifetime supply of minnows from the tackle shop—if you bought them for $76 each.

I also question the practice of fishing with shrimp. Think about the situation. Shrimp cost $6 per pound. Fish cost $3 per pound. This is the same economic formula that produced the federal deficit. The more bites you get, the farther you go into the hole.

Just to show you how bad it can be, solve this sample problem. Feel free to use a calculator.

"If the bait is twice as expensive as the fish, and every fish eats one large shrimp, how long would it take two fishermen with bad credit to go broke?"

The answer is, "Fishermen with bad credit are already broke." But since money rarely matters to fishermen, they could fish as long as they wanted.

A popular bait among saltwater fishermen is the squid. I haven't the foggiest notion how to gather squid for bait, but I suspect it's easy. Anything that ugly probably commits suicide and washes up on the beach.

Some bait simply has to be bought, but you can save significant amounts by shopping for it at the supermarket. Often, people are surprised at some of the tidbits that will entice fish.

For instance, trout love marshmallows. I'm not sure if salmonids are just party animals or if marshmallows resemble Purina Trout Chow.

Trout even like cheese, which may also resemble Trout Chow, although judging by the smell, it was left in the refrigerator way too long.

Catfishers will find the grocery store a gold mine because that's where a broad selection of chicken innards can be found. Livers, gizzards, and assorted guts are all part of the catfish's diet. Catfish eat chicken guts so that nothing worse will happen to them for the rest of the day.

If fishermen ever quit buying these delicacies, the meat counter would quickly be overwhelmed with surplus innards. Sort of a chicken gut glut.

Another surprising bait is Jell-O. Believe it or not, a blend of biscuit dough and Jell-O will drive carp wild, which is a scary thing to witness.

All you have to do is open a can of biscuit dough, pour dry Jell-O powder on it, then knead until blended. This concoction can then be molded into bite-sized balls for carp. Of course, molding carp into something bite-size takes far more thought and a different kind of fish.

Finally, one of the more versatile baits on a grocery shelf is corn. I've caught an assortment of fish ranging from carp to trout, all on whole kernel corn. I've even heard reports that Green Giant brand corn will catch Coho-ho salmon.

Just kidding.

As the Worm Turns

Artificial worms have slithered into our tackle boxes over the years like night crawlers in a June downpour. Everyone has multiple dozens, and most bass fishermen would rather forget the plugs to their boats than their worm boxes.

I've always wondered why the artificial worm was invented when real ones were available. I have a couple of theories. One guess is that plastic worms were invented by a fisherman's wife, a wife tired of night crawlers in her refrigerator. Or perhaps a wife who unfortunately got up for a late night snack, mistook the worm cup for the yogurt, and ate in the dark to keep from waking the baby.

Likewise, it could have been that the first worm was made to hide in a partner's lunch box, a partner particularly scared of snakes.

Either way, that first worm no doubt induced a strike.

Worm fishing is so different from other bass techniques that the best way to learn is to fish with an expert. But before you go, spend some time learning the language of worm fishing, just so you can understand each other.

Worm fishermen have their own dialect. For instance, there's rigging. Some use Carolina rigs, others Texas rigs. I always wondered though, what do I do in Georgia? Are there Georgia rigs? And why are all the rigs named after Southern states? Is this a conspiracy? If I invented a New Jersey rig, for instance, what would I catch . . . carp?

The techniques for casting even have special names, like flippin' and pitchin'. And they weren't as easy for me to learn as you might think. By the time I'd mastered flippin' and pitchin', I was a pro at spittin' and cussin'.

I first thought nothing could be simpler than outfitting myself for worm fishing. I mean, what else is there but a worm, a hook, and a sinker?

Well, once I looked into it, all sorts of variations surfaced.

For example, worms come in more sizes, colors, and flavors than Baskin Robbins ice cream and cost more to boot.

Just to be sure I had all the possibilities covered, I bought a pack of each color and scent. Now my tackle box emits so many conflicting odors it smells like a dumpster.

Maybe that explains why the Missus sets my worm box out on the sidewalk every Tuesday. Either that or she's still mad about the yogurt ordeal.

Some of these odors are particularly rank. I guess these are for guys practicing catch and release. After all, you wouldn't want a fish with dumpster breath in your livewell.

Despite the proliferation of flavors, some have been overlooked. For instance, what about black pepper? Any fish that picks it up would no doubt swallow it when he sneezes.

And did you ever see the names on these worms? Slug, grub, pumpkinseed, watermelon, gourd—it's a wonder they aren't sold at the Feed & Seed Store. Sometimes I forget whether I'm fishing or farming.

And then there are the bubble gum worms. I guess bass are supposed to chew on these for some time.

A lot of questions come to mind when I ponder bubble gum worms. Do bass ever try to blow bubbles with them? If so, do they float to the surface? When the bubbles pop, how do the fish get them off their faces without fingers? And do other bass ever step in bubble gum worms by accident?

One of the newer worms on the market has a strip on one side that looks like Velcro. The idea is that it will snag on the bass's lip and give you more time to set the hook. I'm not sure if even this is enough for me. I need one with a zipper.

Worm sizes range from grub to snake. With the really big ones, bass seem to strike in self-defense. Either that or the worm grabs them . . . probably that Velcro strip.

Another type I've tried was called a Do-Nuthin worm. The first pack I bought must have been the wrong kind. What I got were Catch-Nuthin worms.

Why would anyone want a Do-Nuthin worm anyway? Shouldn't

worms do something? Or are fish just that lazy? Probably any fish that lazy doesn't even eat.

No doubt the part of worm fishing that gives me the most trouble is setting the hook. Talk to three people on how to do this, and you'll get four answers. I've been told to set the hook as soon as I feel the fish, or to crank down the slack line and then set the hook, or even let him hold it until he swims off. It sounds easier to break into Fort Knox than into the mouth of a bass.

One of my friends suggested to cut down on missed strikes that I fish a short line. If it gets much shorter, though, I can gig them.

And I use sharp hooks, too; you know, the kind with a Japanese name that sounds like somebody sneezed.

Hook manufacturers these days are trying to help the guys like me. One offers hooks that are chemically sharpened. Another has designed a hook that "strikes back." What I really need is a hook that picks fights.

One thing that took me forever to get used to was the way bream grab a worm by the tail. I jerked so often that most of the local panfish now suffer from whiplash.

I also have trouble with bait-casting gear. Some people, like me, appear to be genetically impaired for bait-casting. I've made more bird nests than the entire cuckoo population of Switzerland.

After all these years, I'm still not accurate casting with a bait-caster. Of course, nothing ever flew straight coming out of a bird nest.

Another area I'm beginning to learn about is all the gadgets developed especially for worm fishermen.

The odds and ends are countless. Painted sinkers to match the worm. Colored swivels. Hooks with worm holders. Bent hooks. Scent. Glitter. There are more variables here than in Einstein's Theory of Relativity.

Many fishermen even use rattles to liven up their worms, the fishing equivalent of walking a high school band through the library.

And then there are fifty types of worm juice. Some come in their own cups, which I regret looks too much like my no-spill coffee mug. After my buddy accidentally switched the two, I learned why Maxwell House hasn't entered the fish-scent business and why Berkley doesn't make coffee.

Although I must admit, when we did catch fish, I never saw them close their eyes.

Since then, I've also thought about what worm juice should taste like. Most of the things bass eat look mighty unappealing. Don't you think they might appreciate something like T-bone flavor or cheesecake?

But I draw the line with some gadgets. For instance, the guy at the tackle shop tried to sell me a worm welder for on-the-spot repair. I didn't buy it. Instead, I'll just save all the broken ones until I have a bunch, then take the whole pile of them over to Mr. Goodworm.

All in all, worm fishing has turned into a complex sport. It would be lots easier just to put a storage cooler in my basement and go back to using night crawlers. Either that or quit buying yogurt.

Do You Have Striper Fever?

Since the first striper was landlocked, fishermen have been waterlogged fighting fog, rain, and spray off the bow to pursue these fish. Cold temperatures and cloud cover just seem to spur them to the boat ramp even earlier in the day.

The anglers just described have striper fever. It's a highly contagious disease, usually caught with spinning gear.

With all its other programs and problems, the federal government has chosen to let the fishing ranks treat themselves. And the place to start any cure is by diagnosing the problem.

Many fail to recognize striper fever when it first sets in. They may forget and leave their kids at the launching ramp, or throw the boat in gear to chase schooling fish, flipping the youngsters over the stern. Back on land, they may even give single relatives extravagant gifts, such as guided striper trips for two. The worst part is, these are just the early symptoms.

To ask yourself, "Do I have striper fever?" take this test. Answer truthfully, skip no questions and waste no time, unless of course the stripers are in the midst of their spawning run, in which case you should wait three weeks.

THE STRIPER FEVER TEST

1. The sound of gulls diving causes you to reach for:
    A. The boat ignition B. A fishing rod C. An umbrella
2. The last time you spent $200 on a tank, it was for:
    A. Minnows B. Gas C. A septic system
3. Most of your reels are filled with:
    A. 14 lb. test line B. 10 lb. test line C. Cobwebs

4. Your most effective technique for locating stripers is:

A. Following contours on a topo map B. Following gulls C. Following striper guides

5. You usually get your bait by:

A. Throwing casting nets B. Jigging with gold hooks C. Handing someone ten bucks

6. Stripers are known for their sharp:

A. Teeth B. Gills C. Wit

7. Striper fishermen are known for their dull:

A. Hooks B. Fish stories C. Partners

8. When a big striper takes off on his first run, the best thing you can do is:

A. Give him line B. Chase him with the boat C. Alert the Coast Guard, pack a lunch, and hope your kidneys hold up

9. The best way to clean a striper is:

A. With an electric knife B. With the help of someone who knows how C. Bubble bath

10. The last time you saw a large "blip" on your sonar, you had:

A. Found stripers B. Passed over a gar C. Run aground

11. The biggest striper ever put in your boat was:

A. Larger than your youngest child B. The same size as your youngest child C. Caught by your youngest child

12. When stripers are feeding at night, you generally are:

A. Trolling for them B. Using live bait C. Sleeping

13. So far, the specialized equipment you have purchased for striper fishing has cost you:

A. Over $5,000 B. Between $1,000 and $5,000 C. About $3.98

14. The local striper club has nicknamed you:

A. Striper-swiper B. Big Dawg C. Wimpy

15. Based upon your past experiences, your chances of catching a large striper are:

A. High B. Fair C. Equivalent to receiving a lightning strike

16. When the game warden spots you fishing, he usually:

A. Checks you for the limit B. Includes you in his creel survey C. Shakes his head and keeps going

17. When you come home from striper fishing, the neighborhood kids:

A. Line up to look at your catch B. Run to get their parents C. Yell, "Hey, what's your excuse this time?"

18. If they wrote your biography, the part about your striper fishing skills would be covered in:

A. A chapter B. A page C. A footnote

19. On your last winter striper trip, you caught:

A. A 20-pounder B. A 10-pounder C. A cold

20. The most prominent item on your windshield is:

A. A striper decal B. A fishing permit C. A dead bug

Now, to calculate your score, give each answer "A" two points, each answer "B" one point, and each answer "C" no points. Add up your total to take your temperature.

A score of 35-40 definitely says striper fever has struck and is stripping line. You may be too far gone to break free, but maybe you can loosen your drag a bit. Try switching to hybrid bass for brief intervals to lessen your dependence on the pure strain.

If you scored 25-34, striper fever is setting in, and antidotes should be considered. The best remedy, as severe as it sounds, would be motor trouble. For a somewhat less severe treatment, let all your reels backlash. As a final resort, carry utility bills in your pocket. Reality tends to be sobering.

Scores of 5-24 fall squarely in the safety zone. You might get a tad flushed with stripers, but then, anyone with a pulse does.

Finally, a few of you might have scored less than five. This indicates you either have no pulse or else have never been striper fishing. In either case, an encounter with a striper will remedy the situation.

I strongly recommend annually repeating this test. Striper fever has a way of sneaking up on you.

Small, but Game

Getting the Jump on Squirrels

For many hunters, the early squirrel season is the kickoff event to another year of hunting—time to oil the gun, dust off the shells, and make up new excuses for an empty game bag.

The early season offers many challenges, coming as it does on the tail-end of summer. In particular, the cooler temperatures of autumn have yet to chill the ambitions of the bug world.

A biologist once told me that there were more species of insects than any other in the family of animals. I'm not sure how many insect species there are, but during early squirrel season, I've inhaled at least half of them.

Spiders seem to get ready for the opening day of squirrel season by spinning sticky webs about eye level. I don't know if they're pestering me or trying to catch some of those insects before I can inhale them.

Snakes also ply their trade during the early season. I once stood motionless beneath a hickory watching the morning sun rise to highlight squirrels overhead. Meanwhile, a copperhead watched the sun rise to highlight a squirrel hunter overhead—way overhead.

One good thing about squirrel hunting is that you need little equipment to do it, probably nothing more than a gun, shells, and a fifty-gallon drum of insect repellent.

Many hunters claim they most enjoy the challenge of hunting squirrels with a .22 rifle. Not me. I've always preferred hunting squirrels that didn't have a rifle.

The standard weapon for the squirrel hunter is a shotgun loaded with No. fives. That's supposed to be a shot size, not a shell quantity.

Many a hunter entered the sport with a single-barrel 20-gauge, looking for squirrels in a nearby hardwood stand. There's something nostalgic about single-shot guns and the need to reload between misses.

Some hunters bypass squirrels as unchallenging, but a squirrel in the wild is nothing like his freeloading cousin that hangs out in city parks. Wild squirrels can escape quicker than Houdini with a master key.

One of a squirrel's favorite tricks is to circle the tree. As you move around, so does he, keeping the trunk between you. I'm not sure how the squirrel knows where I am without looking. Maybe he hears me humming "Ring Around the Rosie."

Another squirrel trick is to lie flat on a limb to escape detection. Many hunters know that if you shoot the limb, the concussion will drop the squirrel. At least, that's what they claimed to be aiming at when they missed.

Squirrels also sometimes freeze upright on the limb, thinking you'll not notice. And you might not have except for the nervous twitch of their tails, something biologists may someday link to excessive caffeine consumption.

Every hunter has his favorite technique, but I've always found the keys to sneaking up on squirrels are to move slowly, step quietly, and dress to blend in. This last part has become easy enough. If camouflage were any more effective than it is now, you'd have to stay awake to avoid becoming a den tree.

Squirrels can also be called in. A squirrel call makes a raspy sound much like a hunter hacking to clear his throat of a forest spider. I always wondered if squirrels mistook this for another squirrel's bark or if they were coming in for a good laugh.

Another successful technique involves finding a hickory tree with fresh cuttings underneath and waiting for the squirrels to arrive. Of course, you should look closely beforehand to confirm that it's the squirrels doing the cutting and not some Post Grape Nuts fans looking for the taste of wild hickory nuts.

Many of our mountain hardwood stands have old logging roads. These make excellent trails for sneaking up on squirrels, unless of course you meet a logging truck.

Probably the most unusual technique doesn't even involve the use of a gun. I once saw my dad twist a squirrel out of a den tree using a limber stick with a forked end. He ran it into the den, turning it until it had tangled with the hairs in the squirrel's tail, and by the look on Dad's face, I think he would have gladly traded a squirrel in the hand for two in the bush.

Once you have a mess of squirrels, you might find dressing them can be difficult, simply because squirrel hair is fine and sticks to the meat. About the most effective method I've found to dress squirrels is to get someone else to do it.

One unappetizing feature of a dressed squirrel is that it bears strong resemblance to a rat, something you might not want to mention just as dinner guests bite into a fried squirrel leg.

Squirrel meat mostly comes from the legs, and in all honesty, my favorite part of a squirrel dinner is homemade biscuits with squirrel gravy. Partly, this might be because even one squirrel is enough for gravy.

As a final note, keep in mind that little on a squirrel goes to waste, and that even applies to the tails. The Mepps spinner company buys them for making tails on their spinners, paying in cash or reimbursing you with lures. One question I'd like for Mepps to answer, though. Do their squirrel-tail spinners just cast well or do these lures have a natural inclination for hardwoods?

Dove Strategies and How They Think of Them

What, you ask, is so complex about dove hunting? You just sit in a field, wait for one to fly by, then shoot it. If you believe that, you will also believe that all it takes to split an atom is a very sharp knife.

Think about it a bit longer, and you will realize it's not that simple.

First, consider the bird. Doves fly so fast their shadows can't keep up. Their flight paths weave to the extent that trying to lead one is like tracing a noodle through a plate of spaghetti with a crooked fork.

Who trains these birds? I can't decide whether they've been to Top Gun or crop-dusting school.

Probably Top Gun. I've noticed that doves often fly in squadrons. One of their maneuvers I call "The Eight-Dove Weave." Any number of doves can perform this feat; it just looks like eight.

In it, they fly up to the edge of the field in a straight line, and as soon as the first hunter aims, they scramble. Intermingling at high speeds like this, they can almost twist the barrel of any gun that tries to track them.

Dove behavior can puzzle the average mind. For instance, I never see doves in quantity, except on opening day. It's as if they sit on wires in pairs until opening day, then congregate on the field. Could it be that opening day is their big social event of the year? Could they also be wondering if we just drive up and down the road in pairs, and only get out in bunches on opening day?

With all their dives, dips, and dodges, it's no wonder doves are difficult to hit. But that isn't their only defense.

Doves also play with hunters' minds. One of their tricks is to taunt hunters by landing on power lines, the equivalent of a kid on base sticking his tongue out at whoever is "it" in a game of tag. According to a power-line repairman I know, not all hunters show restraint, or else they snap under pressure.

I would never personally stoop so low as to shoot a bird on a wire, but I do experiment with other ways to improve my shooting percentage. I even tried decoys but noticed that most often doves fly over hunters when their backs are turned. So now I carry an inflatable hunter to hunt behind. To make him more realistic, I set him under a power line.

Another trick doves use to particularly taunt hunters is to circle back through a field they have just successfully navigated. No possible instinct or behavioral trait will explain this maneuver except the one the doves offer themselves by the sound of their wings, a whistling that goes like this, "Hee-Hee-Hee-Hee-Hee-Hee."

The doves themselves are not the only concern for a hunter; all kinds of things go wrong in a dove field. For example, your gun can jam. Not just a little. I'm talking rock solid with the action ajar and a live shell inside and enough doves over the field that your dog starts to make snide remarks.

And have you noticed that every pollinating weed in the world blooms during dove season? Last year, my blind was in a patch of goldenrod. Immediately, my eyes began to water and I developed a cough. To counter it, I took antihistamines, but all they did was make me tired. Had I been any more sneezy, sleepy, or dopey, Snow White would have shown up.

The heat can even make hunters delirious. Staring into the horizon, gnats may look like incoming doves. I've seen hunters aim and shoot. This wouldn't have been so bad, but they field-dressed them, too.

The heat apparently can also fuse the pellets together in your shells. Really. How else can you explain your average if you're not shooting slugs?

Missing birds is part of the sport, but I'm among the worst. Every year Winchester sends me a Thank You note.

Even my daughter gets into the act. I took her on opening day last year so she could get a feel for the sport. After one of my particularly long dry spells, she asked, "Daddy, once we empty all these shells, do we get to go home?"

Shells are most often blamed for our misses, but the probability of this many bad loads is slim. You see, misses are never fired as single shots. Misses are always fired in trios. This has become part of the opening day ritual in most fields, resembling an ancient hunter's chant that sounds like, "Bang-Bang-Bang. Cuss-Cuss-Cuss. Bang-Bang-Bang. Cuss-Cuss-Cuss."

Obviously, these natives all shoot automatics. The single-barrel chant only goes, "Bang-Cuss."

If we missed all the time, though, most of us would quit. Actually, hits and misses run in streaks. When you're on, the streak can be so hot you want to run out and buy a lottery ticket. When you're cold, however, your luck can be so foul you're afraid to drive home.

Since it takes me a long time to get a bird down, I hate to lose any that are hit. That's why I carry my trusty bird dog, Clayton Joe. That and because I feed him all year so he ought to do something.

Actually, Clayton is impatient. Whenever I shoot, he runs out to find a bird. If one doesn't fall, he steals one. Some year, I ought to break him of this habit. Or at least teach him to be more discreet.

As a result, I'm always nervous when a game warden comes into our field. It's not because I do anything illegal; it's that with Clayton stealing birds, I can't keep track of them. The last thing I want is to be thrown in jail with too many of someone else's birds. And they don't throw dogs in jail, even though I have suggested as much.

Once I even tried controlling Clayton by putting him on a three-foot check cord and hooking the toe of my boot through a loop on the end. I planned on letting him go only when I hit.

Unfortunately, Clayton reaches top speed in exactly three feet. I am still working on taking my second shot while hopping through a field on one leg behind a Brittany with a stolen dove in his mouth.

Not all my stories speak so highly of Clayton Joe. One year, when it was my turn to bring the doughnuts, Clayton and I were driving to the field well before first light. I stopped at a convenience store for coffee, leaving the doughnuts on the back seat of my Datsun and Clayton on the front floor. As I poured coffee, the smell reminded me of my lapse of sanity, and I rushed to the car to see a Brittany with a doughnut box on his head.

Of course I chewed him out for chewing up the doughnuts. And also as you would expect, the sugar affected his hunting.

Best day he ever had.

Now we go out for doughnuts every year. I just wish he would quit going round and round on that stool.

Besides a good dog, every dove hunter carries lots of stuff into the field. Even me. Coolers, stools, portable blinds . . . I probably bring too much. In fact, my buddies suggested I either get my Brittany to wear saddle bags or teach a sled dog to retrieve.

Hunters take everything but confidence. Otherwise why the extra box of shells?

All things considered, dove hunting may be the most complex outdoor activity there is, with the possible exception of teaching a Brittany to crawl through weeds on his belly with a stolen dove in his mouth.

Throw Me into the Brier Patch

The cottontail rabbit ranks as one of our most hunted species. On occasion, some are even found.

These rabbits elude hunters for many reasons, but the fact that many of us actually do dress like Elmer Fudd is not one of them.

For starters, rabbits know how to use cover, and every one has his own bag of tricks. Some sources even say that when rabbits are caught, they have been known to exclaim, "Please don't throw me in that brier patch!"

Whether true or not, hunters are cautioned not to fall for this trick.

But rabbits have plenty of other tricks. For instance, at the first hint of danger, a rabbit will freeze, sitting tight until forced from cover. Then when pressed, it will burst forth like the squirt you get from stomping a fast food ketchup packet.

Zigzagging quickly through dense brush, a cottontail presents a small target. Shooting a rabbit on the move is about as easy as knocking down a hummingbird with a marshmallow.

Another trick rabbits use is to circle when pursued. Besides keeping them on familiar ground, this technique allows them to cross their own trails and confuse dogs and hunters alike. In a real pinch, they've been known to dive into holes. The rabbits, not the hunters.

Rabbit habitat—try that one three times quickly—usually consists of a combination of brush, weeds, ditches, burrows, and fencerows. In other words, places that commonly give you the urge to mow, burn, or bulldoze.

Diminishing habitat is in fact a problem rabbits have had to contend with over the years. The checkerboard pattern of small farm fields has given way to vast open expanses more suitable to large equipment. This is because a rabbit can turn around in a much smaller space than a Deere.

The best place to find a rabbit is on an edge, where two types of cover come together. For instance, a hedgerow along a grain field offers food and cover, and a rabbit can readily access both at the edge. To take another perspective, it's the same reason you wouldn't want your TV too far from your kitchen, especially if you risked being eaten by hawks as you traveled back and forth, although that would liven up Monday Night Football.

That's just the reason for the love affair rabbits have with cover. The little critters support a number of predators such as foxes, coyotes, cats, owls, and hawks. It could be that rabbits are occasionally found on open ground, but not by you and it's a mistake they are only allowed to make once.

Rabbits are widely distributed in part because of their prolific nature. Consider for a moment that two rabbits breed, yielding the average litter of four. Assuming half females, these two breed with litters of four, yielding eight. Before long, there's sixteen, thirty-two, sixty-four, and so on. This is Mother Nature's version of the pyramid scheme, which would be illegal if any of them were making money.

In pursuit of rabbits, most hunters prefer shotguns with "open chokes," a phrase that makes no sense once you think about it.

One reason for rabbit hunting's popularity is that it's a good sport for beginners, particularly compared to hunting ducks or upland birds. For starters, identification is rarely a problem since nothing on a farm has ears that big except a mule. And if your kid accidentally shoots one of those, he has worse problems than just identification. Try finding that recipe in one of your wild game cookbooks.

Many a hunter began following the dogs afield even before he could carry a gun. In fact, some hunters will tell you they had as much fun then as they do now when they can shoot. The honest ones will tell you they even killed about as many rabbits.

For rabbit hunting, the dog of choice is the beagle. Few dogs pack as much personality into such a small package. I've often wondered if beagles didn't start out years ago as bigger dogs, then just wore themselves down to nubs.

Every beagle differs according to how fresh a scent is required before it will take chase. Some will run a trail so cold they'll chase the mailman as he delivers hunting magazines carrying pictures of rabbits.

Each of these dogs has its own voice, and connoisseurs of the race have coined terms to describe the various barks and howls. For instance, a rapid, frantic bark is referred to as a chop mouth. A dog that speaks in long notes, like a yodel, is called a bawl mouth. But not all tags are complimentary. A dog that likes his own voice and barks whether he has a trail or not is called Rush Limbaugh.

By listening closely to the dogs, you can even tell how close they are to the rabbit and which direction it's heading, unless you misread that earlier tip and dived into a hole.

Hunters differ on the ideal number of beagles to have running at one time. Some like a brace of beagles while others prefer large numbers. Personally, I love to hear the music made by a pack of beagles in pursuit. On a crisp winter morning, a pack of beagles hot on a rabbit's trail sounds prettier than the Mormon Tabernacle Choir, who can't sing worth a hoot when running through thick brush.

In summary, rabbit hunting offers something for everyone, whether it's the youngster just out to follow the hounds or the sportsman in love with the chase. Besides, it's one of the few instances when you can follow a pack of yapping dogs and not be in trouble with the neighborhood cat owners.

Man Attacked by Dead Goose

The *National Intruder* wanted this story, until they learned that it's true and doesn't involve aliens.

Normally, dead geese don't attack people. If they did, Labrador retrievers would be even more popular, and someone would have gotten rich selling electric goose zappers to hang in your yard. So you can surmise that this is a rare event and one that the victim probably wished had remained a secret.

You see, most goose hunters are macho sorts that take no great pride in having been beaten up by a dead goose. That's why I've changed the victim's name. That and the fact that he outweighs me by at least fifty pounds.

The story was told to me by a hunting buddy of the victim with the introduction, "You won't believe what happened to Ralph . . . " As an indication of my journalistic integrity, I didn't believe it. So I asked Ralph. He confirmed the story when he responded, "Who told you that sack of lies? So help me, I'll kill him!"

Which brings us back to Ralph, an avid goose hunter whose day began innocently enough, something unusual for him. He was huddled in a pit, in a cornfield, in the midwestern flyway, when the sun crept over the horizon. Other pits were scattered around the field, and in one of these pits huddled another key player in the story. All the rest of the pits were filled with witnesses.

The details at this point are muddled, probably confused in the hysteria that set in afterward for the uninvolved, but at some point things took a turn for the worse when some geese came by. Had they not, Ralph would have had a pretty decent day.

A number of the geese tried to land for breakfast and guns started firing. Ralph spotted a goose veering off to the right, led it, and shot.

That's when it happened. Somewhere to Ralph's left, another hunter connected, and the goose folded up and crashed toward earth. Unfortunately, Ralph happened to be on the earth at the time.

As Ralph turned to his left to line up a second shot, the guilty goose, which happened to be dead, lined up on Ralph. Catching Ralph from the blind side, the goose effectively got his attention. In short, it hit him square on the noggin and knocked him silly. Some of Ralph's friends think that given Ralph's demeanor, this may not have been the first goose to hit him.

In case you have not looked at a goose lately, they are much bigger than parakeets and when flying swiftly toward earth can pack quite a wallop. This kamikaze dislocated Ralph's shoulder and successfully sidelined him for the day.

Ralph at this point had several much bigger dilemmas. For starters, he had to find a doctor trained in treating people struck by dead geese. This is a specialty few are schooled in, mostly because not many doctors can resist laughing and screeching, "You were hit by a WHAT?"

Next, Ralph somehow had to file the insurance claim. This is probably tougher than it sounds, even under the Clinton Plan. Few insurance forms have a box to be checked that reads "Struck by a dead goose." As a result, Ralph had to check "Other."

No doubt you've heard how commonly people file fraudulent insurance claims, and those that are checked "Other" must be scrutinized. Believe it or not, insurance investigators are not regularly trained in determining whether people are faking being struck by a dead goose. Ever since Joe Friday retired, it has been difficult to find an investigator capable of asking with a straight face, "You were struck by a WHAT?"

Also, the agent would need to be especially skilled in asking verifying questions like, "OK, sir, are you sure it wasn't a possum?" and, "I see, you're right, possums rarely fly in V-formation. Could it have been a terrapin?" and, "Yes, you're right, terrapins don't fly in flocks. And you said that was a goose with a G not an M?"

Many of us were also concerned that Ralph might never goose hunt again. Paranoia of dead goose attacks might have crippled the hunting spirit of a number of hunters, but so far, Ralph has shown no signs of it.

I have concluded that it's just like falling off a horse. At some point, a hunter has to face climbing back into the pit, and the sooner the better.

And it's not just the dead geese, but the other hunters he must face as well. Few can resist yelling across the field once the shooting stops, "Hey, Ralph, look out for that dead goose!"

Finally, there is one last problem, and it's mine, not Ralph's. At some point in time, I could find myself in a pit, in a cornfield, in a midwestern flyway, sitting next to Ralph. By then he will have read this, as will all his buddies since I am sending them copies, and as soon as the shooting stops, he will probably have an uncontrollable urge to beat me with a dead goose.

But then again, it might be worth it should Ralph turn out to be an alien. The *National Intruder* would love that story.

Jackelopes
or Better

The Jackelope Hunt

Beanpole Boggs and I had headed cross-country on our annual big-game expedition. Usually, I try to pick up a rental car when we cross the Mississippi. Driving into small Western towns with an Eastern license plate is like walking into a Masonic lodge wearing a sign on your back that says "Kick Me."

Anyway, Beanpole and I were turned around, if not lost, when the two-lane rutted trail called State Road 171 entered a small town named after the one casualty on Lewis and Clark's trip west. The sign said, "Population 51," and there were three bars, a post office, and a gas station. The post office and gas station were under one roof, a good indication of these folks' priorities. One bar for every seventeen residents spelled a tough town come Saturday night.

We pulled the truck into the gravel parking lot, and twelve miles of dust caught up to us, swirling in from behind in a cloud. Choking, coughing, and slapping dust off our clothes, we picked a door and went in.

The gloom temporarily blinded us. Squinting, I could see a figure lumber off a stool and lean on the counter. About six feet eight inches, three hundred pounds, and unshaven, he looked like an offensive lineman banned from the NFL for chronic unnecessary roughness.

He bellowed at us, "You want something or what?"

"Man," whispered Beanpole. "This is some tough post office."

"Yeah," I replied. "Let's be sure to stay out of the bars."

As I wondered about the life span of farm dogs on his mail route, Beanpole engaged the postmaster in conversation.

"Well, we were looking for a place to hunt animals."

"The bar's full of them. Anything else?"

"Could I get a Coke?" Beanpole asked.

"Next door. This is a post office and a gas station. We sell gas and stamps. Which one you want?"

Beanpole thought for a minute. "I'll take a stamp."

While Beanpole counted out the change, I looked out the door at the three bars. Not a Volvo in sight.

We walked back out together, watching behind us.

"Well," I asked, "should we try The Mangy Moose, The Dead Skunk, or Shorty's?"

It was no contest.

Seconds later, we were standing face to face with the bartender in Shorty's. A pleasant fellow, he was about six feet four inches tall.

"Hello, boys. What'll ya have?"

"Cokes. Is Shorty around?" I asked.

"You're talkin' to him," replied Shorty, putting two Cokes on the bar.

"Why do they call you Shorty?" asked Beanpole, tipping back the Coke and guzzling about half of it.

"I'm the smallest in my family," Shorty chuckled. "You should see my older brother."

"He's not a mailman, is he?"

"Oh, you've met him then. I try to stay away from him this time of the month. All that government stuff, you know, farm payments, social security, food stamps. It comes on the first, and he has to go to every house on the route. Gets grouchy as a badger on hot pavement."

"Hadn't noticed," I said. "Say, do you know where we could hunt some mule deer? Or maybe an antelope or two?"

Shorty looked us over. "You're not from around here, are you?"

He squinted at us when he said this, reminding me of an old fishing buddy, Buck. Buck always got this look when he was minnow fishing for bass and his bobber started bouncing, a look that said there's a big one playing with the bait.

"No," said Beanpole. "We're not from around here."

"Well, it's hard to get hunting permission out here when you're not a local." Shorty wiped the bar with a rag as he talked. From the pulsing of his biceps, I wondered if he were sanding or washing.

"But you could be in luck," he said. "I know a rancher who's having trouble with a jackelope infestation."

"Jackelopes?" asked Beanpole.

"Oh, yeah. Thick." Shorty shuddered.

"What's a jackelope?" asked Beanpole.

Shorty's squint changed to a gleam, the same gleam that Buck always got when the bobber started off and he began to feed line. Two local boys moved over to the bar and silently traded empty bottles for full ones. They sat down in hearing range like school boys at story time.

"Jackelope's a sort of a cross, a high-bred I think they call them. Out here, the jackrabbit range overlaps with the antelope range. Somehow, they crossed." Then he pointed to the far wall where a rabbit head hung, a rabbit head with a four-point rack.

Beanpole walked over and stared.

"Do they get any bigger than this one?" asked Beanpole.

"Sometimes. And during the rut, those buck rabbits will tear up every sage on the prairie. Anybody with yard shrubs can kiss them good-bye. On still fall nights when the moon's full, you can hear them, CLACK-CLACK-CLACK, banging antlers together to see who is the top rabbit, er . . . jackelope."

Beanpole came back to his stool. "How do you hunt them?"

"I like to sit on a knoll overlooking a crossing," said Shorty. "This time of year, they're scattered, just before the fall rut. Their antlers are probably coming out of velvet, and they'll be feeding heavy to get ready for winter. On a good crossing, you can see twenty, maybe thirty a day."

"Wow!" said Beanpole. "That would be some good shootin', huh, Jim?"

"Huh," I offered back, watching Shorty watch me.

"What kind of load should I use?" asked Beanpole.

"What are you carrying?" asked Shorty.

"A .25-06 with 100 grain bullets," answered Beanpole.

"Perfect," answered Shorty. "Just perfect. And you?"

"Buckshot," I said. "Ten gauge."

Shorty turned back to Beanpole abruptly. "Let me draw you a map out to this ranch."

"Great," replied Beanpole.

While Shorty scribbled, Beanpole glanced back at the mount on the wall, his head filled with visions of jackelopes charging through the brush.

Shorty handed Beanpole the map. "Anything else you boys need to know?"

Beanpole thought briefly. You could almost see the hamsters turning the wheels inside.

"Yeah, as a matter of fact, there is. Can you call these things in? That would liven it up a bit."

Shorty leaned in toward Beanpole and lowered his voice. His eyebrows tilted slightly, another expression I had seen before. It was the look of concentration Buck always had after the bait had been taken, swallowed, and it was time to set the hook.

"Well, you can call them with a rabbit call. The bucks come in thinking it's a doe. But you don't want to do that. Not around here. Too many things come in thinking they're going to eat rabbit, particularly the . . . "

"The what?" asked Beanpole.

"The grizzlyote. Meanest animal alive. Head of the grizzly on one end and the head of a coyote on the other."

"With a head on each end, how do they know which way to go?" asked Beanpole.

"They don't. Always arguing over it. That's what makes them so mean."

Luckily, this was when the screen door to the bar slammed shut and two strangers stood squinting, trying to adjust to the gloom. Shorty called out, "Come on over. You boys aren't from around here, are you?"

Cliff's Ride

"As soon as I squeezed the trigger, I knew I had missed," Cliff said, telling the story while it was still fresh.

"A six-pointer was trying to slip by, and when he eased up to step out from behind a broad old beech, I aimed and fired. Then, a limb about two feet over his shoulder cracked and swung like a pendulum, taunting me, the way they will back at camp just before they cut off my shirttail and hang it for all the world to gloat over."

Cliff finished, and I almost expected him to ask for a cigarette and firing squad. Being a newcomer to the Crooked Creek Hunt Club was tough enough with the practical jokes and teasing. It was about as much fun as being buried up to your neck in a sandpile. Subtract one shirttail, and the sandpile becomes an anthill.

Since Cliff was the youngest member and I was his sponsor, I felt obligated to help.

I thought back over the shirttail ritual. One wall of the clubhouse was adorned with shirttails from the first-year members who'd made the mistake of missing. Red-and-black flannel flags flapped every time the door swung open.

As if that weren't enough, the unfortunate few were forever referred to as Rookies. Gus, our senior Rookie, had now been in the club thirty-two years.

Cliff started talking to himself. "Maybe I ought to just quit. Go join the Mucky Swamp Hole Club. They take misfits, you know, guys with crooked barrels. Maybe they would at least let me cook, then I could be near deer hunters. Maybe even clean their dog pens. Nah, I'm not good enough for that."

106

Cliff kept mumbling, going downhill fast.

"Calm down now, it may not be so bad."

"I don't see how. Everyone heard the shot," moaned Cliff.

"Maybe," I countered, "but how many know you missed?"

"What?"

"They only cut your shirttail off if you miss, right?"

"Well, yes. How do they verify a hit?" he asked.

"All you have to do is produce some evidence, a blood trail for instance."

Cliff's chin sank into his chest. "I already looked," he said. "There's not a drop to be found anywhere."

I glanced left and right quickly. "They don't know that, at least, not yet."

Cliff brightened. "Maybe there is a blood trail. I didn't look that close." He winked. "How do I do it?"

"Well, I don't usually suggest this sort of thing, but this shirttail business can get ugly. You know where we dress our deer, the rack? The leaves under it are covered with blood. If you could slip back unseen, then you could load your bag and lay down a trail to the creek. Then, one of our experts on deer behavior will explain how deer head for water when hit and you're in the clear. The trick will be to get there and back without being seen."

The sun was past its peak, and Cliff stared at it, calculating how much time he had before the others began drifting back into camp. He must hike two miles to camp, scoop the leaves, hike back, lay the trail, then be ready with his story when the truck stopped by his stand to pick him up.

"Will you come with me?" he asked.

"What for?"

"I . . . uh . . . it was your idea."

"All right, but let's get it in gear. We've got a lot of ground to cover."

The road back to camp was good fodder for a Jeep advertisement. The ruts disfigured the single lane, cut two feet into the earth by loggers in the Depression years. Frozen and hard, the mud stood in erratic ridges. Wherever the sun slipped between trees and warmed the clay, the surface became slick, like soap on a washboard.

We made good time through the shady patches and slowed to pick our way through the sunny ones. After covering nearly a mile, we heard a dog's high-pitched yodel.

Both of us froze. "Sounds like Colonel," I said. "When he strikes, he runs till he drops."

"There's Missy and Junk Man," I added. "They'll quit before the Colonel will."

The dogs' serenade continued, moving parallel to the road along Crooked Creek. I imagined Cliff's deer picking his way quickly through the deadfall and briers, followed by three snuffling hounds. After a couple minutes, only the Colonel kept singing, moving downstream toward the beaver ponds known as the Duck Holes.

We quickened our pace again, remembering what we were up to, when we saw a pickup in the road ahead. The tailgate was down, and an open dog box big enough for six hounds filled the truck bed.

"That's where the drivers hoped the dogs would come out," I said. "Looks like they were two-thirds right."

Junk Man and Missy stood tongue-hanging tired in the road bed, having left the chase to the Colonel. Suddenly we heard footsteps.

"Quick, hide," I whispered, and before I could stop him, Cliff dived into the dark recesses of the dog box.

"Hey, did you see the Colonel?" yelled Arnie between gasps for breath. He dragged up to the tailgate followed by his brother Bennie, and both sat down to catch their breaths.

"No, sounded like he was headed for the Duck Holes," I offered with a quick glance into the dog box.

"Dadgummit, we'll be in there all night hunting him," wheezed Arnie.

"Maybe not," said Bennie between pants. "It's three miles to the bridge." Pant. Wheeze. "Maybe we can beat him there."

"Well, it's worth a try if we hurry," gasped Arnie. Before I could argue, he was shoving Missy and Junk Man into the dog box and popping it shut.

"You coming, Jim?"

"Oh yes, wouldn't miss this for the world."

Arnie and Bennie loved action. As long as I could remember, they had been drivers for the Crooked Creek Hunt Club. Wiry as hounds themselves, they could keep pace with the dogs until a deer jumped. They knew where to head off the race and collect the dogs and how to get there first. The rutted roads were more familiar to Arnie than the trail to his refrigerator.

Likewise, he drove the roads knowing every hole, bump, and rut, managing to hit them all.

Arnie shifted into four-wheel drive before we started, and when he popped the clutch and jumped the first rut, multiple thumps were heard back in the dog box.

Our ride out would bring new fame to Disney World if they could duplicate it. Only my iron grip on the arm rest kept me from banging my head.

Farther back, I continued to hear bumps, thumps, and toenails scratching and clawing. I wondered if Cliff had his boots off.

"Isn't this tough on the dogs?" I asked.

"Nah," laughed Arnie. "They're used to it. We do this about twice a week."

As if to prove it, he gunned it, jumped the next rut, and fishtailed around the next turn. The dog box sounded like a popcorn popper with all the elbows and knees bouncing on the plywood. Coming face to face with a dark green pickup, the color that says "Game Warden," we slid to a stop just shy of his front bumper.

I listened for moans in the back but, hearing none, figured Cliff was out cold.

The warden walked up and leaned in Arnie's window.

"Where's the fire?" he drawled.

"Got a hound running for the Duck Holes," offered Arnie. "We're just trying to head him off."

"Any deer? I heard a shot."

"No," said Arnie. "At least not us. We heard it, too. Sounded like that young fellow we put on the stand this morning."

"Well," said the warden, "we had an anonymous tip of some illegal doe kill. You don't mind if I check out the dog box?"

"No problem," said Arnie. "Those pups are too pooped to get out."

Before the warden could move and Arnie open his door, I jumped out.

"Let me open it for you. Keep your seat, Arnie."

We got to the tailgate simultaneously. I dropped it and opened the dog-box doors. The stench of hot, wet hounds struck us as we leaned in to look. Three noses struggled through the opening, gasping for fresh air. One had a mustache under it.

The warden's eyes widened. He glanced from Cliff's pale face to mine and back, several times. Finally, he spoke.

"I have heard of your initiations over here on Crooked Creek, but this one takes the cake."

"Yes, well . . . we can't let just everyone in," I muttered sheepishly.

"Does he have to run with the hounds, too?"

"No," I managed to laugh weakly. "Just ride with them."

Our conversation had been low, so neither Arnie nor Bennie could hear. I shoved the three heads back into the box, the one with the mustache most resistant. Then I closed the tailgate and got back in the truck while the warden looked under the bed.

"What did he say?" asked Bennie.

"Oh, just small talk," I answered.

We waited patiently. Finally, the warden came back up and leaned into Arnie's window again.

"Everything OK?" asked Arnie.

"Yeah, well, except for one thing."

I stiffened. Surely, he wouldn't tell. But then again, he probably thought they knew already. I started preparing a story, searching for an explanation.

Before I was ready, Arnie asked, "What's that?"

The warden looked first at him, then slowly at Bennie and me.

"Those are some U-G-L-Y dogs!"

Then he laughed and walked back to his car, chuckling at his joke. Arnie and Bennie looked at me. I just shrugged.

"Well," I said, "at least it's not against the law. Come on, we've got a couple more miles of frozen ruts between here and the Duck Holes. Let's get bouncin'!"

Talkin' Turkey

Turkey hunters wait for opening day of the spring season with such anticipation that many argue this day should be specially recognized. In many states it is. They call it April Fool's Day.

Were it not for this excitement, hunters would be unable to roll out of bed in the middle of the night. Turkey hunters rise so early that it was actually a turkey hunter who first witnessed that the early bird gets the worm. And that hunter was on his way home.

Of course, rising early has its downside. A hunter quickly learns, for instance, what a tight choke really has to do with turkey hunting. It's the grip his spouse gets on his throat when the alarm wakes the baby at three a.m.

Turkey hunting can appear complex to the novice. For instance, a beginner once asked me at an outdoor equipment show where you aimed to keep shot out of the stuffing. I just laughed and shook my head.

How should I know?

Some hunters get so caught up in the sport, however, that they take it to extremes. A friend of mine went out and bought his son a special first grade reader. It started out, "Run, Kee Kee Run."

The hunter finally saw the error in his ways when report cards came home. Oh, the reading grades were fine, but the kid got low scores in conduct for yelping in class.

One skill that helps every turkey hunter is marksmanship. When I started, my aim was so poor I couldn't have hit a turkey dinner with a fork.

Speaking of dinners, did you ever wonder who shot the turkey for the first Thanksgiving at Plymouth Rock? Judging from the choke on those Pilgrims' muzzleloaders, I'd bet on the Indians.

Because turkeys see so well, hunters go to extremes to stay hidden. Clothing manufacturers have conducted years of research to help them out. Camouflage patterns these days are so effective that during the early spring it's difficult not to become a nest.

And although many hunters prefer simple blinds, others opt for something far more elaborate. I saw one blind so sophisticated I'm sure it was Venetian. It even had a drawstring.

Turkeys are really fascinating birds; just think about their habits of calling, roosting, and strutting. Of course, their strut is nothing compared to what you can see at a game check station from a hunter who just bagged one.

My call isn't that great, but it always amazes me that turkeys in the wild really don't sound so good themselves. I once heard a hen that sounded like she was gargling gravel in an oil drum. And a vet I know passed up a shot to treat the bird for laryngitis.

It's odd too that gobblers on the roost answer an owl hoot. I think it's because gobblers actually know the answer to the question, "Who?" When the answer is me, their response sounds like the turkey version of a chuckle.

Many turkey calls are now on the market, and every hunter has his favorite. But did you ever contemplate what the guy was thinking when he invented the wing-bone call? I mean, why the wing bone? My guess is that it's the only leftover turkey part anyone would want to put in his mouth.

When my luck is really running sour, I have a special call I use. It's made from the wishbone.

Corn-cob strikers are another interesting item. Probably these originated from some turkey hunter making use of available materials and spare time while in an outhouse.

Some people have trouble deciding just how much calling is enough. You know you're calling too much when Ma Bell sends you a bill.

I know that when I first started, I called far too much. After a morning filled with yelps and putts, I'd come out of the woods feeling like Arnold Palmer.

But when I started, I didn't even know what a putt was. My best guess was that it was a noise made in the dim light of morning by a hunter who walked into a spider web with his mouth open. Except it usually sounded like "Pfft" and had a bunch of other words behind it.

112

I've always had trouble mastering the different calls. The best yelp I ever let out was one time I backed into a cat brier while answering nature's call. On second thought, it might have been more appropriately referred to as a fly-down cackle.

I should probably confess that even with all my knowledge and experience, I still find turkey hunting a challenge. Gobblers generally seem to be just a tad smarter than I am. In fact, I get skunked so regularly that my wife has started dousing me with tomato juice the minute I get home.

It's frustrating. I'd switch to fishing, but I have no idea what a turkey would bite.

Bear Necessities

Backwoods travelers learn many skills, some not because they plan to use them, but because they hope not to. In this category, you can include administering first aid, living without toilet paper, and running into bears.

Learning about bears requires not only picking up new ideas, but forgetting a few preconceived notions. For instance, when I was growing up, I thought three kinds of bears roamed the woods: black bears, grizzly bears, and Big Ol' Bears. Black bears ate honey, grizzly bears ate fish, and Big Ol' Bears ate people.

Usually Big Ol' Bears showed up in late night stories told under the questionable notion of pumping a kid full of scary stories to put him to sleep. The story usually went like this:

"There we were, minding our own business, when suddenly out stepped a Big Ol' Bear!"

Just as an aside, "minding our own business" was also a key phrase, and along the way I decided this was a prerequisite to trouble and something I have since tried to avoid.

As most naturalists know, bears are actually quite tolerant, and if you want proof, look at the tale of Goldilocks. She broke into the bears' house, ate their food, damaged their chairs, slept in their beds, and was then caught on the premises. The bears had her outnumbered three to one and let her off without so much as a warning ticket. Even Goldilocks must hold bears in high esteem.

Of course, the bear's view of Goldilocks is probably a bit different.

One lesson learned by every student of bear necessities is that bears deserve respect. To have some notion of a bear's majesty, simply go back and read the notes of Lewis and Clark as they traveled to the Pacific. Judging from their comments, the bears chased them across the continent.

Lewis and Clark were in awe of the grizzly's strength and power and encouraged their men not to engage the Great Bear if alone. This was an easy agreement to reach since grizzlies had already encouraged the men to hide in terror, jump into rivers, and run like roaches when the lights go on.

More recently, natural history writers have described the presence of bears as an indicator of wilderness. For an area to be truly wild, they say, a predator of man is required. Maybe so, but I'd bet that's one wilderness experience they were not having when they made this comment.

Still, wilderness travelers need to know how to behave around bears. Experts suggest that if confronted by a bear in open territory, you should roll over and play dead. I have a problem with that. I would hate to spend my last minutes imitating a possum.

Besides, I would probably get a bear that plays with his food.

Lying perfectly still while a bear rolls you back and forth to see if you really are dead would take tremendous self-control, particularly of your bladder.

The worst reaction, according to the experts, is running, since that is the natural reaction of many bear foods, and bears can outrun a race horse. But then again, with the right motivation, so could I.

It has been proven, however, that in most situations, bears will run the other way. So apparently we're either out of season or not all that good to eat.

Of all the bears, the least predictable is the grizzly. All you can really say for sure is that the grizzly tops the food chain, and it's in your best interest to avoid becoming a missing link. Bears are classified as omnivorous, which means they consume plants and animals. In other words, whether it moves or not, they eat it. This is another good reason not to play possum.

A number of things bears eat are rather odd. For instance, grizzlies supposedly eat porcupines. They do this by jumping over them, flipping them from the other end, then scooping out the meat with their paws, thereby avoiding the quills. Porcupines are viewed by grizzlies as meals that come with their own toothpicks.

This raises an interesting question, namely, would bears perform similar operations with armadillos, sort of like possum on the half shell?

Insects form another important part of a bear's diet. When ants go on a picnic, it's the bears that show up.

Even berries are part of the bear's diet. Somehow I have difficulty picturing something as big as a bear picking something as small as berries. That must be like watching a ballet performed by Jackie Gleason.

Bears' feeding habits often create problems for park rangers, particularly when the bears feed at the dump. It just proves that even bears enjoy dining out.

But of all the bears' skills and inclinations, the most admirable is their fishing ability, and none are better at this than grizzlies. I'm not sure if they obey all the game laws, but I'd wager that no warden ever asked a grizzly for his license.

One sign of their intelligence is that they only go after the premium fish, such as salmon. You never hear about bears lining up around a carp pond.

The grizzly's love for fishing is just further proof of its intelligence. Think about it. You work for a living, and grizzlies spend their summers fishing in Alaska. Which species sounds smarter?

In many ways, bears have it made. They're the biggest animals in the woods, and they can do whatever they want. They even get to hibernate all winter. I could enjoy a long nap like that. Of course, with my luck, the phone would ring.

But did you ever wonder what a bear with insomnia does all winter? He can't count sheep; that would just make him hungry.

The ultimate danger in bear country is to come between a female bear and her cubs. The reason for this is simple. If you'd been stuck in a cave all winter with two kids, you'd be grouchy, too.

Were Lewis and Clark alive today, they could speak from experience about bear encounters. Of course, if the conversation took place in bear country, they would probably talk about the bear's ability to outrun race horses while they quietly tied your shoelaces together. No doubt they learned that the question is not always whether you can outrun the bear.

Skills for the Hills

Updating Weather Folklore

Without the weather, every barber shop in America would slip into silence, a change of events some might consider an improvement. But we dwell on the weather because it influences our society beyond picnics, car washes, and outdoor weddings. It always has.

For some reason, though, we give past generations credit for being better forecasters than we are now, simply because of their knowledge of natural signs. But if that were true, why do we find so many of them frozen inside glaciers?

I can hear it now. Some caveman named Og says, "Honey, it's such a nice day, I think I'll go kill a mammoth." And then came that one little cloud. By the time Og realizes what happened, he's thawing out in the Smithsonian.

Millions of dollars are spent to launch satellites, to man weather stations, and to monitor radar just to tell people it will rain, when they could wait another twenty-four hours and see for themselves.

The worst part is that weather forecasters often are wrong, and no one seems to care. Maybe that's why television stations hire likable people that no one will want to blame and make them say things like, "Remember yesterday when we said it might rain? Well, it DID!"

But society has progressed somewhat. For awhile, our goal was to control the weather. What a waste that would have been. Even if we could have done it, we would never have gotten everyone to agree on what they wanted.

Heaven forbid if the Weather Controller's job was filled through general election. I can see it now: "What a coincidence," said The Incumbent. "No rain in sight between now and the election."

So instead of controlling the weather, we just try to anticipate it. One of the oldest tools we use is *The Farmer's Almanac,* a booklet now more than two hundred years old.

Did you ever wonder how *The Farmer's Almanac* forecasts the weather? Well, according to the editors, they have a proven formula locked away in a black box. This formula reportedly uses the sun, moon, and other events to predict the weather.

I doubt it. I'll bet in that black box there's just a slip of paper that reads, "When in doubt, forecast a fifty percent chance of rain. In other words, it might rain and it might not."

Weather concerns, however, predate even the *Almanac.* The earliest recorded prediction was probably Noah's, although he was working on insider information. As long as it took to build the ark, you have to wonder if his neighbors tired of hearing Noah say, "Hmmm, looks like rain."

In the absence of insider information, folks learned to use natural signs to predict the weather, though interpretation is always needed.

For instance, if you see a rope twist, it's supposed to rain. Either that or you've been reading too many Stephen King novels.

Another favorite was "Red sky at night, sailor's delight." Hah. Not the sailors I know. A red sky doesn't come close to a weekend pass.

Consider some other old-time sayings. For instance, "When terrapins head for high ground, look for rain." If by chance they proceed to climb a tree, look for a lot.

And, "If cattle lie down when put to pasture, expect rain." But how do you know they're not just pooped?

The most famous predictor, of course, is the bit about the groundhog and his shadow. But aren't we giving that furry critter too much credit? What makes us think groundhogs even notice things like shadows? Maybe he was bending over to look at a bug.

And then there's the old saw about March weather, "In like a lamb, out like a lion." What happens if March rambles in like a possum?

Similar to the early attempts to control weather, I've recently tried using folklore to my own advantage. Last fall, I spent several days painting wide brown bands on woolly worms. It didn't help a bit.

Some folklore has been given different interpretations in modern times. Early settlers said that if the kingfisher disappears, expect fine weather. Today you should first check your neighborhood for a trigger-happy kid with a BB gun.

Old-timers also thought that if toads showed up in great numbers, it would rain. Nowadays it could just mean that you left your porch light on and they're after the bugs.

Actually, we are probably creating weather folklore right now that future generations will use.

Whereas in the past we predicted a harsh winter if there were lots of nuts in the hickory trees, now we'll expect a harsh winter if there's lots of nuts at the hardware store buying snow shovels.

Also, you know it will be a harsh winter if the price of antifreeze skyrockets.

Still, animals will continue to be our primary source of clues about the weather.

Since house pets will be the most common animals around, they will provide the most useful clues. For example, if your hamster stuffs all his food into his cheeks and digs to the bottom of his litter, get in a closet quick.

Or if your cat comes home when you call, then either the weather's going to get worse or it's not garbage day.

As always, however, many people will remain skeptical that anyone can predict the weather. It was true in Noah's day, and it is true now. There will always be doubters. But even if you're among this group, I'd batten down the hatches should you happen to notice animals lining up in pairs by your bass boat.

The Winter of Our Discount Tent

Winter may be the best time of year for camping in many parts of the country. Should you be among those who avoid the sport for safety reasons, allow me to put it in perspective. Winter camping typically involves nothing more life-threatening than forging on once the potato chips run out.

That is, as long as you're prepared. Camping experts will tell you that survival becomes a serious issue when you're disoriented, ill-equipped, or unprepared, which covers me about 80 percent of the time.

Actually, I'm just being modest. I have considerable experience camping in places where winter temperatures drop well below zero. Of course, I did it during the summer.

The key to comfort in winter camping is properly maintaining your body temperature. You can do this with your choice of clothes, tent, and sleeping bag, and by regularly sneaking around the bend to the Ranger's house.

Up until the new synthetics came along, down was the preferred substance for insulating sleeping bags. Partly this was because down fibers trap air extremely well and partly because using the whole duck made the sleeping bag too lumpy.

Certain weather conditions can make winter camping uncomfortable. For example, consider wind. Winter wind has teeth; probably that's where you get frostbite.

Weather forecasters spend a lot of time discussing wind chill this time of the year. The origin of this concept has been traced to a northern weather forecaster looking for a good excuse not to take out the garbage.

To prepare themselves for weather changes, veteran winter campers have learned to watch wildlife for signs of change. For example, one sign of approaching bad weather is extraordinary wildlife activity, particularly if the animals are carrying luggage.

Humidity is another factor that affects your comfort, and being wet will add a whole new dimension to winter camping. Not only are you colder, but it also becomes more difficult to start a fire. In fact, the only thing that becomes simpler in wet, cold weather is talking everyone into going home.

Should you accidentally get wet in subfreezing temperatures, rolling in snow can actually blot up the excess water before it soaks in. It also enables you to do a decent impression of the Abominable Snowman.

Perhaps the highlight of winter camping is the food. At the end of a long, cold day, there's nothing like a hot dinner. But few campers like to spend hours cooking with a lot of different pots and pans to clean later. The solution to this is to serve dishes that only require boiling water, so you have only one large pot to heat and none to clean. This does have its drawbacks though. On a long trip, even the uncomplaining camper may tire of oatmeal, rice, and grits, particularly when mixed.

High-energy foods are usually recommended for the winter camper to help keep up his body temperature. For example, you can find granola bars that would be perfect, except at ten degrees they have the texture of a brick. Still, that's better than eating rice cakes, which admittedly stay soft but have the *flavor* of a brick.

Another good feature of winter camping is that you can take along foods that would spoil in the summer. Sometimes you can even find campsites with snowdrifts nearby, which lets you stash your perishables in the snow, much like having your refrigerator except the little light never comes on.

Furthermore, on winter camping trips, rarely will it get warm enough after dark for bugs to fly. Of course, that does make it more difficult to explain all those black specks in your food.

And on those frosty mornings, there's something special about the aroma of freshly brewed coffee. Unfortunately, the guys I camp with have no appreciation for how much I enjoy this. I believe their exact words were, "If you want coffee, get up and boil the water yourself. And by the way, we still have some of that grits, oatmeal, and rice mix that you brought along."

Winter campers generally have a few tricks that make life simpler. For example, a roll of cardboard coated with candle wax makes a good fire starter. Then again, so does a butane torch.

Because heat is so important, winter campers take extra care in waterproofing matches. Some use waterproof tubes, pill bottles, or Ziploc bags. Some even dip their matches in melted paraffin to be waterproofed. When I tried it, I did such a good job dipping the matches that they were also fireproof.

A fire-starting trick that should be abandoned is lighting sticks doused with gasoline, unless you have an intense desire to pass through life without eyebrows.

One problem I have with starting fires is that my matches are always in an inside pocket. Since I dress in layers during the winter, I have to undress to get to the matches, which makes little sense when you consider that I'm building the fire to get warm.

Finally, there's something else I've never understood. Why is it nature always calls on the coldest nights when I'm warm and settled into my sleeping bag?

That's definitely one time that call forwarding would be worth the money.

Go Take a Hike

Walking, according to recent statistics, is one of the most popular outdoor activities. I didn't realize that many people knew where they were going.

On second thought, that may explain the popularity of walking: knowing where you're going is not a prerequisite.

Walking has long been a popular pastime. Charles William Beebe, American scientist and explorer, once said, "A first walk in any new country is one of the things which makes life on this planet worth being grateful for." That and a chance later to get off your feet.

Walking provides good exercise because all parts of your body get involved. Your feet flex, your legs stride, and your arms swing, and all the while your brain's telling you to stop while your eyes look for a place to sit.

Your mental health also benefits from your walking. If someone's getting on your nerves, walk away and you'll feel better instantly.

Besides the health benefits, walking is good for the economy, particularly the companies that make shoes, compasses, and emergency first aid kits.

Sociologists have noted that the importance of an activity is often reflected by the number of words that are available to describe the activity. For instance, you can pick up a thesaurus and find at least ten to fifteen synonyms for walk. The difference in most of these is how fast the walker goes and whether he has any notion of where he's headed.

Take, for instance, "meander." If you meander, you aren't in a hurry and have no idea where you're going. I meander a lot, even when I'm not walking.

Walking the dog is a variation of meandering, since the dog usually leads and only he knows where the next hydrant is located.

"Promenade" is a term I especially like. I think this one refers to a square dancer on a hike.

If you "ramble," you're exploring aimlessly. That is, you're covering ground with a poor sense of direction.

Richard Jefferies, English naturalist and novelist, probably was a rambler. He once wrote, "you cannot walk fast very long on a footpath." I've found that to be true. Sooner or later, I leave the trail, get lost, and start banging into trees.

To "traverse," you must travel across an obstacle or overcome adversity, something like crawling out of your sleeping bag before daylight on a cold morning to start the coffee. Then you streak back before your bag gets cold.

John Kieran, ornithologist and scholar, observed, "Pasture land makes easy walking. The cows and horses pave the way." Not only that, they also leave trail markers.

Any time is good for walking. Once I participated in a group hike after dark, by the light of the full moon. For some reason, though, we were constantly losing the unmarried couples, particularly the teenagers, but all the married people were able to keep up. Figure that one.

Technique can determine how much you enjoy walking. For instance, finding the proper rhythm makes walking far easier. All it takes is practice to find the pace at which your breathing and motion come easiest. I found mine in a Lazy-Boy recliner.

The idea is to walk steadily. Constant starting and stopping makes about as much sense as a quick jog to McDonald's.

One technique popular on steep terrain involves shifting weight from one leg to the other with a brief pause in between. This technique is known as the rest step. Of course, it is not as popular as the rest stop.

Proper foot care is also important, and when it comes to foot care, prevention is the sole issue.

The most common problem is improper footwear. Even better than putting your best foot forward is to have two equally good feet.

New boots can be tough on tender feet. A good way to break them in is to put them on and clump around your house or apartment for short periods, unless you live above large neighbors, have wooden floors, and are most active after midnight. In this case, walking could prove detrimental to your health.

Very little special equipment is needed for walking. In fact, you don't even need shoes, as long as you have mud puddles or beach sand, or don't mind chanting EE-OW-EECH as you hike.

Probably the most useful item to take along is your curiosity. And that may also explain why so few people walk their cats.

Henry David Thoreau summed it up best: "A taste for the beautiful is most cultivated out of doors." And nothing tastes like trail dust.

(Dis)Orienteering

Getting lost has never been much of a problem for me; the problem is getting found.

All outdoorsmen, regardless of their pursuit, sooner or later find themselves lost. I have often wondered on the rare occasions it happened to me just where I went wrong. Typically, I decide it was when I opened the door of my truck.

Reasons for getting lost abound. Of course, bad weather leads the list. Blinding storms, moonless nights, and heavy fog can cause even the most experienced woodsman to lose his way. I suppose it's because it becomes so hard to see the bread crumbs.

A number of other excuses can also be identified for getting lost, but since you will have plenty of time to think it over, you might as well come up with your own.

Outdoor manuals provide lots of good advice for people who are lost. Unfortunately, they never have these books with them when it happens.

One of the first tips from these manuals is to determine if you really are lost. Some people apparently have trouble deciding. Here are a few clues:

You know you're lost when, rather than run away, the chipmunks point and snicker. Likewise, take it as a bad sign when you cross paths with a pack of coyotes and they're all wearing bibs. And not only are you lost, but far off the trail should you notice that even the buzzards pack a lunch.

Outdoor manuals also recommend a number of tools for orienteering, starting off with maps. The problem I have with maps as a tool is that they are most useful when you know where you are on the map. But if I knew that, I wouldn't be lost. Never have I come upon a dead tree with a large black X and the words "You Are Here."

The maps recommended most often are those available from the U.S. Geological Survey, called topographic or topo maps. In case you have never seen one, a topo map has contour lines on it. Basically, a contour line shows those points of equal elevation.

In other words, if you are lost on a mountain peak and follow the contour, you will go neither up nor down, thus circling the mountain and returning to the same place, which is probably what you would do if you were lost without a topo map.

When you are lost, some of the outdoor manuals suggest that rather than aiming for a specific point, you should target a baseline, or long boundary that can be more easily identified. Streams and roads are good examples. If you are really turned around, you might consider something larger, like an ocean.

Another piece of advice regularly offered is to carry a compass. This assumes, of course, that you know how to use it. Actually, it would make more sense to me to carry an ex-Marine sergeant.

Regardless of the tools you carry, including maps, compasses, and ex-Marines, sooner or later you will get lost. Then you face an important decision: Do you sit tight and wait for help, or depend upon your own intuition? While you're thinking this one through, keep in mind that it was your intuition that got you lost.

For those who decide to find their own way out, the terrain might lend some clues. For instance, many experts suggest that if you can find a creek or river, you should follow it downstream. I've found that, better yet, if there are fish in the stream, you should look for a really good fishing hole. Typically, someone else always gets there first, and you can just ask them for directions.

That old bit of folklore about moss growing on the north side of the tree rarely helps much, mainly because you will have no idea which side of the tree your truck's on.

One of the oldest methods of navigating is by the stars. Early travelers relied almost solely on this technique, which explains why so many of them got lost. I tried this once and was led three miles out of my way by trying to follow what I thought was the North Star. It turned out to be a satellite, probably one the Russians put there for just that purpose.

Under dire circumstances, hunters can signal for help by firing three shots in the air. This generally works best when you're not under someone's tree stand.

Another method of orienting yourself is called the shadow-stick method. This involves a series of time-consuming maneuvers that consist of marking shadows, plotting lines, and finding true north. I've found it far more effective to set fire to these sticks and hope someone sees the smoke signal.

One experience I have yet to enjoy is to be rescued by a Saint Bernard with a keg under his neck. This seems to me a stunt concocted by Hollywood. In the real world, the rescue team would take the keg, throw a party, and if you're lucky, send out some mutt with a six-pack of RC Colas.

Once you conclude that you cannot find your way, the only solution left is to make the best of a bad situation. This is when most outdoor survival guides get ridiculous. For example, mine says, "Intelligent preparation is the best way to avoid trouble when lost."

If I had intelligently prepared, I wouldn't be lost.

The second idiotic survival tip is that getting lost only becomes an emergency when combined with panic. Now that calms me down.

The third and final tip (I think this is where I slammed the book shut) is to leave word where you will be so someone can find you. I suppose I'm to write a note that reads something like this: "Dear Sir, on Saturday I will be getting lost on Snaggle Tooth Peak, just down the slope from the bare rock outcrop. Please send help."

Survival kits can be bought for these situations, and most outdoor manuals have a list of recommended items so you can assemble your own. Just for convenience, I bought a pre-assembled kit from Lost-R-Us.

The items in survival kits usually serve one of two purposes: either to keep you warm or to provide you with water. If you don't want to carry one of these kits and you get lost, you can survive just as well by heading for the nearest hot tub.

Living off the land has been suggested by some experts, but this one deserves a lot of thought. Some plants that are edible negatively impact the digestive system. Other plants are deadly. That's why I prefer animals.

Not that I really eat them. It's just that there's nothing like a plate full of grubs, grasshoppers, and lizards to remind you that there are things worse than being lost, such as a plate full of grubs, grasshoppers, and lizards.

Finally, having field-tested a number of survival guides and checking lists in my outdoor guides, I've discovered them all lacking.

129

Matches, tarps, and fire starter are nice, but if I'm huddled in a driving rain, shivering in falling temperatures, and waiting on a search party, I'd much prefer to be packing the ultimate in survivor gear—a cellular phone.

You can also get them at Lost-R-Us.

In the Woods Too Long?

Deer hunters learn quickly that when it comes to bagging a deer, there's no substitute for spending time in the woods. This holds true mainly because it is next to impossible to shoot a deer while watching television, unless you have a really long extension cord and keep the volume down.

But as with anything, even deer hunting can be overdone. You can spend so much time in the woods that other aspects of life get neglected, such as generating enough income to buy shells, licenses, and anniversary presents.

In fact, even though it relieves stress, too much deer hunting can shorten your life span, particularly if you have to opt for the shells and license and forego the anniversary present.

Luckily, those who hunt in excess will receive advance notice if they know what to look for. So in hopes of keeping the deer hunter from becoming an endangered species, I have developed a list of signals.

For instance, the more time you spend outside, the more you become one with nature. But you'll know you've been in the woods too long when moss begins to grow on your north side.

Nature will offer signs, too, if you overstay your welcome. When field mice begin to nest in your Fruit of the Looms, you'll know you stayed too long. Another good indicator is that chipmunks start naming their kids after you.

Also, you are too long in the woods should you notice your portable tree stand has sprouted leaves, bloomed, or borne fruit.

Sometimes your best clues come from other people. For example, if you meet another hunter and he offers to buy your gun as an antique, you have been out much too long.

Sure, tramping around the woods is great exercise, but you know you have overdone it when boot companies start sending you Christmas cards.

Another sign that you need a lifestyle change comes when you've eaten so many Beanee Weenees that the aluminum recycling center is named after you and Rolaids tries to hire you as a field tester.

The reactions of people at work should also be considered. For instance, when you notify your boss that you'll be out of work hunting deer until the fifteenth of the month, you know you're in trouble when he asks, "What month?"

It's gotten really bad when you tell him, and he responds in disbelief, "What year?"

Perhaps the best indicators of having stayed in the woods too long are the quirks you develop. For example, when you can find your tree stand in the dark on a moonless night, but you still trip over furniture in your living room, that's a bad sign.

Another bad sign is when your hunting log for one season has more pages than *Moby Dick*.

Even your spending habits will offer hints. You know you've lost track of time when you start buying industrial-sized bottles of insect repellent.

Cold feet are a common companion of the woodsman. Should you catch yourself going to bed with a cold water bottle, ask yourself why.

Another good idea is to check your trigger finger for calluses.

Even the way you dress can say a lot. Take a look in your closet. You know you've been in the woods too long if the only colors are patterns of camouflage.

Of course, you have gone well over the edge when you begin to believe there really is such a thing as a jackelope.

Perhaps the ultimate clue comes at Christmas when someone gives you deerskin gloves, and you think you recognize the hide.

Admittedly, many of the above indicators could be coincidence. Yet there are even stronger signals that you have been out with the deer far too long.

For instance, you should take heed if the first cold snap of fall sends you into rut.

Worse yet, you've been chasing way too many deer if you notice yourself responding to buck lure.

If you sit down at the dinner table and answer every question with a grunt, you're in trouble, and, although it may work well, it's considered poor form to call your kids home by rattling antlers.

Too much time in the woods can be especially hazardous if you notice yourself crossing the street at night, and your first impulse is to freeze in front of car headlights.

Even when you try to act normal, you might still notice small behavior traits that give you away. For example, if you spend a fall Saturday raking leaves, it is not normal to scrape the bark on a few trees just to feel more at home.

Maybe you still think spending too much time in the woods can't be all that bad. Well, think again, because there's more to planning for retirement than planting a tree where you'd like to have a tree stand. You also need to pay for licenses, shells, and, oh yes, anniversary presents.

Kayuk-Yuk-Yuk

Laughing is serious business when you're upside down in a kayak. But I couldn't help it. Here I was, a grown man, flipped like a child's toy in a bathtub, and all I could think of was a repetitive jingle: "Weebles might wobble but they won't fall down . . . " I felt like a flipped weeble.

I entered this kayaking class because I was totally ignorant of the sport. I always pictured kayakers as different—you know, the kind of people who eat yogurt, wild hickory nuts, and possum soup. To show you how wrong I was, my group included a doctor and a lawyer. And neither liked yogurt.

Was I ever reassured to be in the company of a doctor *and* a lawyer. Just think, if I had an accident, not only could I get immediate medical attention, but if something really went wrong, I could instantly sue for malpractice.

By anyone's measuring stick, I was a novice. Kayak sounded to me like a Chinese word for "Gesundheit." For the first thirty minutes of our class, every time the instructor said "kayak," I added, "Bless you." The other students thought I was a priest.

And the sport appeared so simple. You can't misspell kayak, since forward or backward it's the same. The boat takes after the word with little difference on either end, and the paddle has two blades so you don't even have to know which end to put in the water.

But if Perry Mason ever tries to prove kayaking is foolproof, I'll get a summons.

Should any of you consider taking up kayaking, let me offer a few insights and suggestions gleaned from my first two days under water.

134

First, there is no hole in the bottom of a kayak. From a distance, kayakers appear to be wearing the boat like a water float, using their feet to walk on the bottom. This may not be such a bad idea, but today's kayaks have yet to incorporate such a convenience.

Second, the beginning kayaker must learn two classes of maneuvers: those you perform right-side up and those you perform upside down. Of the two, the latter tend to be more important, so let's start there.

Of the upside-down moves, the best to know is the Eskimo roll. This is not an Alaskan breakfast food, but a maneuver designed to put a kayaker upright before the Piece of the Rock group begins negotiations with his next of kin. No doubt my flailings not only could have kept a whole tribe of Eskimos rolling, but brought hysteria to their sled dogs as well.

My standards and the instructor's were not the same on this maneuver. He said you could tell a good kayaker by how well he can Eskimo roll. I argued the true measure of skill was in how well he avoids one.

The second upside-down move of importance is how to bail out. Despite my prowess at this maneuver, someone kept putting me back in and before long I was learning right-side up moves.

Among these are paddle strokes, buddy maneuvers to help right unsuccessful Eskimos, and ferries. When my friends had told me earlier I would cross streams using ferries, I had envisioned a larger boat to load my kayak onto. Unfortunately, the ferry is a crossing maneuver that gives the novice one more chance to talk to fish.

Portage is another term I picked up. It is a French word for walking where even fools fear to tread water.

Kayak equipment and boats are a lesson in themselves. I was put in a Jeti, said to be a forgiving craft. I suspect I was forgiven, but not forgotten. Before it was over, the boat had been dropped, submerged, and run into rocks, logs, sandbars, and very nearly a concrete bridge piling.

By the way, bridges look much different from a kayak. Never before did I realize they have teeth.

Kayaks come in one- and two-person models. I rate two-hole kayaks the same as two-hole outhouses: in principle they sound fine, but I'm not sure it's a place I would want to be with another person.

I never did learn, however, why kayaks are pointed. Was it to skewer rubber rafts or to stick in a mud bank, in the event a novice hits head-on?

And then there's all the gear. The kayaker wears enough gear to make even the beginner suspicious. First, there's the helmet. If good things were about to happen, why would you need a helmet? Second, everyone wears a life vest. Again, just one more reminder to check your insurance policy. Third, most kayakers wear wet suits. Notice a trend here? Finally, no one leaves the bank without a splash skirt to keep the boat from immediately filling with water should it tip. Or should I say, when it tips. If this group of paraphernalia doesn't clue you in on upcoming events, then you're a used-car salesman's dream.

Looking back on my two days under water, several memories stand out. Best of all, I remember how completely kayaking clears the cobwebs from the brain. Each dog-leg in the river requires a different approach, a unique paddle stroke, and total concentration.

One rapid in particular sums up the experience. It wasn't steep enough to be classified a waterfall, more like a kayak disposal. At the top, all I could see were waves, no rocks, no logs, no turns. I figured I could find my way from on top of the waves.

Then, I eased into the current and took off. The kayak didn't bounce over the water so much as it sliced it. The boat had little drag until the waves hit me squarely in the chest. Water splashed over my head and I found myself stretching and blinking away water to see over the waves, stroking hard on the paddle to build speed. Again, splash, stretch, stroke. And again, harder. Then with a final burst, I popped out of the spray into the near silence of a pool.

And then I slumped forward and rested, knowing that nothing else had mattered or entered my mind for the last thirty seconds, not work, not bills, nothing.

Not only does this sport take you away from it all, it imposes a penalty—dunking—if your mind tries to drift back to the office.

After day one on the water, we sat around a television watching a video on kayaking basics. So completely absorbed were we by the action that no one had his mind on work until one of the actors commented, "Out here on the water, you forget your responsibilities, your job, your bills." To which the doctor in the group replied, "You know, until he reminded me, I had." Likewise, so had the rest of us. And we spent the next few minutes looking for the way back to our earlier thoughts.

The Monday morning after my weekend on the water, I awoke stiff, remembering immediately where I had been the two days before. I felt like a kid who had fallen asleep during his own birthday party, only to wake and find his friends and the decorations gone.

I resented being back here with responsibilities, a job, and bills. My only consolation was that the world that had held me so completely was on a river just a short drive away. That, and the fact that I was dry for the first time in two days.

Not Fully Equipped

BALOOIE!

C.SHELBY

Deer Scents and Nonsense

Deer scents and I go back a long ways. Truth is, my friends wish we went back farther—and maybe a little downwind.

But over the years, I've learned a little, experimented a lot and offended a good many. You might be interested in the fruits of my efforts, before they rot.

Every deer scent had one thing in common back in the old days: it stunk. And at the same time, we all believed that the stronger the smell, the more effective the scent. To test this theory, I got the strongest bottle of scent I could find. Problem is, when I dumped it on my boots, it gagged my Odor Eaters.

Trappers were among the first to use scents, and their techniques were straightforward. Put out enough with sufficient strength, and anything with a refined olfactory system will recognize the trap as the *easy* way out.

Hunters, taking advantage of the deer's superior sense of smell, adopted the technique. You could hear them chatting over coffee, "Oh yeah, I hunt to enjoy nature and take in some fresh air," and as soon as they're out of the truck they douse their boots with deer excrement and skunk juice.

In a historical sense, today's deer hunters may have evolved from yesterday's cowboys. The biggest difference is that whereas cowboys died with their boots on, with deer hunters, it could have been their boots that killed them.

But there's a lot about the early days I would like to know more about, such as the unsuccessful attempts to make scents. For instance, did skunk-based scents ever cause a hunter to be chased up a tree by a skunk in rut?

A lot of novices think deer scents only attract. Actually, they also repel. I've used them to keep away bill collectors, vacuum cleaner reps, and even kids selling candy for the high school band.

Deer scents are potent and should only be used by responsible adults. Unfortunately, hunters rarely notice what scents do to others. It's amazing how a guy can sit in a puddle of deer pee for twelve hours, come home, walk into the house and exclaim, "Hoooeee, what's that stinkin' smell?" to which his wife invariably replies either, "My new perfume," or "Your dinner, Twerp!"

In these situations, deer scents undoubtedly create family problems. To test this, walk into a just-cleaned house with that stuff on your boots. No doubt you'll be chased clear out of the territory by a spouse in a rut.

My wife has a great sense of humor, though, and takes it in stride. Of course, she did start using my hunting pants in the off-season to line the hamster's cage. Funnier yet, it took me three seasons to realize it. I guess it was the pocket full of sunflower seeds that finally tipped me off.

Manufacturers, however, have begun to think of ways to reduce these family problems. One has come out with a masking odor designed to get you back into the house. It's available in three scents: Roses, Chocolates, and Cash.

Inside sources say they're planning a scent that smells like a new washer and dryer. This one will even open locked doors if supplemented with rattling techniques, preferably the banging of old washer lids or detergent boxes.

Have you ever thought about all the problems the deer-scent industry must have? Today it's big business, but can you imagine being the first guy wanting to go to factory-scale production and needing a loan to do it? I can hear the banker now. "You want $50,000 so you can bottle and sell *what*?"

And someday I want to tour a production facility, to see how they make deer scent. In my mind, I envision a guy with a cup following deer around and trying to collect the stuff before it hits the ground. No doubt it's the same fellow who follows the elephants when there's a circus in town.

How do they collect this stuff, anyway? Does one guy hold a cup while another puts the hoof of a sleeping deer in a bucket of warm water? All of those guys from summer camp have to be working somewhere.

And think for a minute about their manufacturing problems. Every business has an occasional glitch, but have you ever thought about what might go wrong in a deer-scent factory? Maybe their deer aren't drinking enough water, and volumes decline. What do you do then—force-feed them tea and coffee?

And what about quality control? You want that job?

Industrial accidents are bad in any business, but just picture what could go wrong in a scent factory. I can see the headlines now: "Man Falls Into Vat Of Deer Scent—Co-workers Won't Let Him Out."

With all the regulations coming out of Washington these days, it's surprising that labeling legislation has yet to make it to deer scents. If it had, the bottle might read, "Contains deer urine and other fluids taken from animals with kidney disorders. Handle with caution in elevators, closets, and truck cabs. If spilled on the nose, rinse with Lysol and apply clothespin. Inducing vomiting will not be necessary."

I suspect deer scent is one of those products for which you really don't *want* to know the ingredients.

If you've never bought deer scent before, let me give you a few pointers on the myriad products available. First, you'll notice they come in various types and strengths. You can buy glandular scents that work as sexual attractors, masking scents that work because they smell worse than you do, and "unscents" that make no scent.

Rumor has it that they're working on a camouflage pattern that also makes you look like nothing. That may be okay in the woods or for avoiding work around the house, but you wouldn't want to wear it in a truckstop parking lot.

Some companies even rate their glandular scents for effectiveness, with the strongest being X-rated. It comes with a warning, "For use in tree stands only."

One thing's for sure; the stuff works. You'll hear all kinds of amazing stories about scents. Deer rush scrapes, confront hunters, and snort in defiance. I guess if I had their sense of smell, I'd confront hunters and snort in defiance, too.

You'll also notice that deer scents come in a variety of novel forms, including fluids, solid sticks, and underarm deodorants that may last ten days or even longer. No doubt I would opt for pine scent in that one.

The longest-lasting deer-scent deodorant is a natural stone for underarm use that's effective up to two years. Of course, not many hunters will want to walk around for that long holding rocks under their arms.

Scent holders are also available, even though that really is a misnomer. Unfortunately, they don't hold scent in, they let it out.

Even with all of these product variations, however, there are a few ideas I would like to put in the hopper. How about a scent that changes after dark to smell like Old Spice? Or maybe a scent that attracts deer and repels snakes, chiggers, gnats, and mosquitoes?

Still, even with their recent growth, all is not rosy in the industry. Some hunters have exhibited strange side effects. For instance, one guy in New Jersey reportedly fell asleep in his tree stand while wearing a masking scent. He dreamed he worked for Roto Rooter and proceeded to stuff his shotgun barrel into a knothole to service a squirrel's den. (It all made sense later when it was revealed he was hunting with a pump.)

Scents are becoming just another accepted part of American culture. Someday, I expect to see a cartoon starring Pepe Le Pew, that French skunk, driving down the road with a scented deer hunter hanging from his rear-view mirror.

So It Ain't Broke,
Fix It Anyway

The theory behind equipment maintenance eludes me. Maintenance implies that you are fixing something before it breaks; but if it hasn't broken yet, how do you know what to fix?

Still, I give it my best shot every winter since most of this stuff can be done indoors where it's warm.

Usually, I start with my boat, a rustic craft with a few years on it. To give you an idea of its age, the previous owner painted a name on the stern—*The Santa Maria*.

The first ritual I practice in maintaining my boat is to kick my trailer tires as if this rig were still on the lot. It doesn't serve any particular purpose, but I find it comforting to pretend I don't own it.

When I originally bought my boat and trailer, I asked for every option that would make maintenance easier. So when it came to my trailer, I insisted on buddy bearings. Of course, that was because I thought they came with a buddy to grease them.

Based upon experience, some items are definitely on my annual checklist. For instance, I always have my truck brakes inspected, particularly the emergency brakes, which, by the way, are appropriately named. Let them start slipping on a steep ramp and you will definitely have an emergency.

Another good item to check is your livewell, including your pump, lines, and outlet. One winter my pump cracked and leaked, allowing water to seep into the bottom of the boat whether the pump was running or not. I don't mind giving a fish I've caught room to swim around, but if I'd discovered that leak fifteen minutes later, he would have had the whole boat.

Take a moment to check your safety equipment as well, such as your lights, winch rope, safety straps, and personal flotation devices (PFDs). The law says you need one PFD per person on board, and it has to float. Otherwise, PFD could come to stand for "Pray For Dryland."

If your boat's like mine, it could also use a general cleaning. Last year, I talked my fishing buddy out of smoking in my boat; he switched to smokeless tobacco. Judging from the side of my boat, this year he needs to switch to spitless tobacco.

An often overlooked item for stream fishermen to check is their waders. You might want to check yours for dry rot. There are a number of ways to do this, but one simple way is to fill them with water. Of course, most people do this before they get to the stream.

The next place to turn your attention is to your fishing rods. These deserve going over from end to end. For starters, your line probably needs replacing. After a year on the spool, old line falls off the reel like a Slinkie. Coils drop to the floor in perfect formation, each one remembering exactly where it had been on the reel.

I've never been much of a reel mechanic. Basically, I try to clean out last year's grit to make room for this year's grit.

The rods themselves generally require little attention, just a quick look at the eyes to be sure there are no sharp edges to abrade or cut the line. Besides, as soon as you did anything extensive to your rod, it would get closed in a car door anyway.

Tackle boxes require a different kind of maintenance. Take a look at yours. No doubt the hooks, split shot, and lures you use most often are gone. What you have left is a box full of stuff you never use, because it's all the wrong size, shape, or color. Which raises a good question. Why do you take all that stuff fishing?

Actually, I know the answer because I do it, too. It's self-defense. You never know when a fishing partner will start catching fish on some lure you never use. So you buy all of them, just in case.

The other problem with your tackle box lurks in its bottom. That's where you toss lures when you are in a hurry, and now you have a ball of crankbaits all gnarled up like a fishing booby trap.

Also, you probably have a few used hooks loose in your box, and you might want to spend some time checking them over, particularly if you forgot and left them baited.

Up until now, all this maintenance talk has sounded like drudgery. But repair time offers a bonus as well, since never again will you have so many good excuses to buy new stuff. Depending on who has the checkbook, you might want to address the issue gingerly. One of my favorite approaches is, "Honey, you want me to buy new rubber worms or have these recapped?"

Once in the tackle shop, you're bound to see some new gizmo that's just perfect. Of course, next season it will still be in your box, untouched.

This year, when I made my tackle-shop rounds, I noticed that every lure rattles. I would think that if you got too many of those in the lake at once it would give the fish a headache.

Lures can make just about every sound imaginable now. Besides the rattles, which come in varying volumes, you can also buy electronic baits that grunt, beep, and even blink. Pretty soon, there will be one that sits on a shelf until you walk by and then says, "Psst, hey, Bubba, buy me."

Finally, it never hurts to check your registration, licenses, and boat insurance to be sure they're up to date. It's mighty easy to let them run out. I wonder if anyone has thought about putting a calendar in one of those talking lures and rigging it to say, "Hey, Bubba, your license has expired."

Tinkering

Outdoorsmen are born tinkerers. The genetic material that creates a love for wet dogs and mildewed boat seats also causes these individuals to tinker. Of course, nature has proven a few mutants exist in all species, even man.

Like me, for instance. I'm not much of a tinkerer. Just to show you how bad I am, the last time I charged a battery, I used my Visa.

Like most guys, I started out doing some of my own work. Probably the most complex task I ever tackled was sandblasting an old boat trailer. I used dynamite. Only later did I learn the proper technique. Should you by any chance be considering my approach, I can assure you the dynamite did do quite a number on the trailer, not to mention the cat.

People seem to readily notice my skills, or lack of them. When I first started house hunting, my real estate agent refused to show me anything listed as a "Handyman's Special."

In fact, my wife, Jan, often refers to me as the Plumber's Helper. She says I help keep them employed.

Now, Jan even gets nervous if I stay in the garage too long. Every time she hears a sonic boom, she runs out to see if the garage is still there. I guess it all dates back to the sandblasting incident. She was always real fond of that cat.

But don't get the wrong picture; it isn't like she has no confidence in me at all. Once Jan confided I could probably get rich refinishing antiques if I had the right tools and materials to work with. Of course, she suggested I start with new furniture and a crowbar.

Even my three-year-old has caught on. He has renamed all my tools. The hammer he refers to as the BANG-DANGIT. The drill is the WEEE-YEOW! And it took us two weeks to make him forget the name of my lug wrench.

Originally, I thought I might someday be good at tinkering, because when it comes to repairing stuff, I'm patient. Unfortunately, it's usually at Memorial Hospital.

During one recent stay, Jan asked if I could use some reading material. I responded that a fix-it book might be appropriate and I would let her pick out the one she thought I could put to best use. She brought me a Red Cross manual.

My lack of tinkering aptitude applies especially to boats. You know how some guys get their outboards to purr like a contented animal? Well, mine does to an extent, if you consider the San Diego Chicken contented.

I've seen guys that can fine-tune an outboard so it always starts on the first pull. On mine, the best I can hope for on the first pull is that the rope doesn't break.

Let's face it. It's embarrassing when you walk into a store, a lady waits on you, and you quickly discover she knows more about boat repair than you do. And it's even worse when you realize you entered the wrong door by mistake and you're in the beauty salon!

Maybe I'm paranoid, but I think repairmen are starting to watch for me. When by chance they see me in the hardware store, I've noticed they follow me around the aisles to see what I buy. If it's anything remotely related to repairs, they will tail me home and wait in my driveway. It's the fix-it trade's version of ambulance chasing.

Before I began to rely heavily upon repairmen, Jan kept a back-up file of names sorted by project. For instance, under outboard repair you could find a list of pawn shops, under electrical work was the number for EMS, and for some reason, under trailers was the number for Small Claims Court.

Some of the mechanics I use are better than others. For instance, I once thought I had the perfect truck mechanic, Mr. Goodgrief. But then I saw that his shop was surrounded by a giant junkyard. Did you ever notice how many small garages are next to junkyards? It makes you wonder, which one feeds on the other? I got nervous just thinking about it.

One reason I have always tried to avoid taking stuff to mechanics is because their bills are so high. And mechanics are always grouchy, like they have headaches. Do you think it could be altitude sickness?

Recently, I started taking all my boat work to Uncle Sam's Marina, even though he is expensive. I guess the reason I like his shop is because it's so classy. When he closes up at night and releases his guard dogs, he turns loose a pack of poodles.

And talk about plush. His roach motels take reservations.

Of course, he claims the reason he charges a lot is to pay for all his expensive tools. But how much can a few BANG-DANGITS and a WEEE-YEOW! cost?

Even though I'm not very good with tools, I still love them and am constantly coming up with new and versatile uses that even my mechanically inclined friends have failed to realize. Did you know, for instance, that a flat file makes a pretty nifty splint?

And every Christmas, tools are on my list. Last year, I asked Jan for a new vise. She suggested I was too silly for wine, too married for women, and too tone deaf for song.

Finally, she did relent and gave me state-of-the-art equipment—Nerf Tools.

I have come to the conclusion, however, that even routine maintenance is beyond my comprehension. The last time I attempted some routine maintenance, it was greasing the wheels on my trailer. It went in easily enough, but I had a hard time keeping it between the treads.

Being the outdoorsman that I am, I keep a lot of stuff around and once in a blue moon try working on it. As a result, my basement is a showplace of sorts; but then, so is Ripley's Believe It or Not.

I can just imagine my relatives arguing over all the stuff not specifically addressed in my will.

"You take the boat . . . "

"Oh, no, you don't. Jim did some of his own boat work. You take it . . . "

"No way. Tell you what. You take the boat and I'll throw in his truck . . . "

Eventually, I'll have to take a class or something to improve my tinkering skills, simply because outdoor gear always breaks in remote areas at the wrong time.

Last winter, my truck broke down again. Talk about remote—as I was walking out I came across wagon tracks from the early settlers. And they were fresh.

Also, there seems to be something in the atmosphere that causes trucks to break down at the same time babies choose to be born, either when it is least convenient or in the middle of the night.

Now I understand why doctors smack babies when they're born. I kick my truck for the same reason.

All things considered, I would probably come out ahead if I gave up tinkering altogether, not just in terms of dollars and cents, but also in peace of mind.

Besides, it's the least I can do now for the cat.

Equipment for Camping in Style

Camping has evolved over the years until there is a form to satisfy everyone. Whether you like sand in your soup or critters in your caviar, you will find a style of camping to fit your taste, or lack of it.

If luxury is your drive, just jump behind the wheel of a recreational vehicle, or as often abbreviated, RV.

RVs used to look like rolling sardine cans. They've come a long way, although they stopped often for gas. Nowadays, RVs have more luxuries than our first house. Come to think of it, they cost more than our first house.

Having never actually owned an RV, there's a lot about them I don't know. For instance, what happens when you flush the toilet in an RV? Until someone tells me, I'm going to be very careful following these things down the interstate.

The part I think I'd like best about an RV, though, is that it's a form of camping where setting up is as simple as putting it into park.

With the growing popularity of RVs, most campgrounds have added electrical and water hookups, so now you have running water and television. We've taken camping from wondering whether to take along soap to wondering whether to watch your Soaps.

And to help bring those stations into remote locations, some RVs even have their own miniature satellite dishes. When Monday night baseball comes on, you can hear the cry throughout the campground: "Circle the wagons, boys—here come the Cleveland Indians!"

About the only obvious disadvantage of RVs is that they can be inconvenient to drive around on errands. Perhaps that's why we see

RVs pulling small cars around for just that purpose. Still, it seems odd having gone from pulling trailers with our cars to pulling cars with our trailers.

Not that everyone has given up on pulling trailers. Pop-up campers seem to be especially popular with families having small kids. I guess that's because kids are likely to pop up at all hours of the night.

Pop-up campers have the advantage of collapsing into a form that's easy to tow. You just have to be careful you don't fold it up with the kids inside.

With many inventions, I wonder, "Who thought of that?" If I had to guess, I'd bet pop-up campers were invented by an accordion player.

Another form of self-contained camper is the truck camper. It's almost like being a turtle, except you go faster—but with considerably worse gas mileage.

Truck bed covers are another alternative that at least keep you from having to sleep on the cold, hard ground. Instead, you get to sleep on the cold, hard truck bed.

Tents, however, are quite another story. With a tent, your bed is only as comfortable as the rock you sleep on. And all the campgrounds I've stayed in cover the tent sites with pea gravel. I have no idea why, unless it's for those people who forgot and left their rocks at home.

Every tent also has its own personality. Our old family tent leaked like a scout-camp rowboat. Actually, this proved both bad and good. The bad news was that you often woke up wet. The good news was that you always knew what the weather was like.

Tents today even come in different shapes. You can buy domes, geodesics, even pup tents. I wondered where pup tents got their names until I bought one. That first night, I slept like a dog.

The ultimate form of camping, however, is sleeping under the stars—no roof, no burdens, no cares, no comfort.

When you sleep in the open, you're really at nature's mercy. Actually, I've learned that nature has no mercy, just a sense of humor. Out in the open with no shelter, you get to live just like the early settlers, who by the way, had an average life span of thirty-five years.

Sleeping out under the stars usually puts me in a contemplative mood. After a long day of fighting heat, gnats, and sudden cloudbursts, as I finally lie down and wiggle around in search of a dry spot in my sleeping bag, I find myself staring up into the far reaches of space and asking myself, "I wonder what the monthly payment is on an RV?"

Bringing Up
the Rear

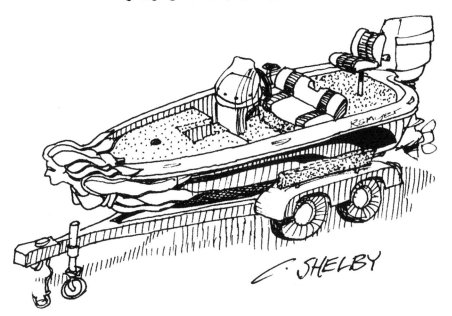

Survival Skills for the Uncivilized

Outdoorsmen sometimes find themselves wandering into strange environs, harsh and uncomfortable to their weathered souls. The usual landmarks are gone. Panic wells up in their throats, and only choking fear holds it in check. These places have many names, most unsuited for children's ears, but generally they are referred to as High-Class Joints.

Fine restaurants lure many an outdoorsman and spouse on special occasions, usually for a Christmas dinner, Mother's Day, or an anniversary. Yet the minute he steps inside, an outdoorsman knows his every move is being watched and judged. Just one false step, one wrong move, and the critics will be on him like a pack of jackals.

But it doesn't have to be that way for you. To venture into a high-class joint and emerge unscathed, you only need to know two things.

First, you have to be able to recognize a high-class joint. Second, you must know the rules of etiquette that apply within these premises.

Let's start with the first one. To help you distinguish between types of restaurants, let's look at Pierre's Pointe, a high-class joint, and Dewey's Duck-Inn, a low-class joint.

One of the first indicators is the parking lot out front. Vehicles say a lot about a restaurant. I once saw an eating place surrounded by European sports cars. One had a bumper sticker that read, "This is Mercedes country—on a clear night you can hear a Volvo depreciate."

Bet your Browning boots that was a high-class joint.

High-class joints also tend to be secluded. They are always in alcoves, or behind, above, or below other buildings and harder to find than a hook dropped on a night-fishing trip. Don't expect a neon sign that blinks, "EAT!"

Another clue is what happens in the parking lot. Usually, some youngster in a black jacket will greet you, then take your keys and your car. At a high-class joint like Pierre's, you'll get the car back.

Inside the restaurant, the first thing you'll see is that you can't see. That's the part that still confuses me. If the food's good, you eat it in the dark. In Dewey's Duck-Inn, you eat burgers and Rolaids under a spotlight. It should be the other way around.

After you're immersed in darkness, Pierre himself will scare you witless by stepping up to greet you when you least expect it. That's all Pierre does. A clerk will then check your reservation, and if you have one, show you to your seat. A good rule of thumb is that in a low-class joint, the most direction you'll ever get is "Park it over there!"

Pierre also has more employees than customers. Figure it takes one guide, four waiters, a water boy, one table sweeper, two cooks, and three dishwashers just to fix your dinner. That also explains why the food costs so much.

On a table at Pierre's, there will be enough utensils to serve Ulysses' army. Three forks, two spoons, two knives, a glass of water, one for wine, a cup for coffee, one plate for looks (since they always put your food on another one in the kitchen), and a saucer for butter are standard fare. At Dewey's, you would expect to eat from a paper plate and drink from a Mason jar, and when you sit down the last guy's food will still be on the table.

Both high-class and low-class joints have lots of food on the menus. But at Dewey's, you actually see food *on* the menu.

Old food dominates Pierre's menu and sells at a premium, whereas Dewey has to mark down his old food and run it on special. Twenty-year old wines and month-old steaks are apparently worth more than day-old chili.

Not only does Pierre keep track of his food's age, but he's mighty proud of its birthplace, too. Gulf shrimp, Dover sole, and Maine lobster are a few examples. At Dewey's, most patrons are afraid to learn where the food's been and are mostly interested in where it's going.

One trick of Pierre's is renaming food so that it sounds better. Pierre's squab is really pigeon, his Cornish hen is just a little chicken, and his blackened mahi-mahi is fish. Any fish that gets blackened at Dewey's is an accident.

Fire can be an important indicator of restaurant quality. In a high-class place, such as Pierre's, they set fire to your food at the table. If, however, they set fire to your food in the kitchen, then you're at Dewey's. This latter instance is what Dewey and others in the trade refer to as the Poor Man's Microwave.

Pierre also likes to serve food raw. After charging you the way he does, you would think Pierre could at least cook it. But no. Sushi, oysters on the half shell, and raw vegetables abound.

Finally, at Pierre's Pointe, your food arrives in shifts called courses. Maybe that's done to keep all his help busy shuffling back and forth. At Dewey's Duck-Inn, meals are designed by architects to fit on one plate and your check comes with the food.

Using these abundant signs, you should now be able to identify a high-class joint once you find it. The next trick is turning on the etiquette.

Five rules will get you through any dinner with ease.

First, never order ketchup in a high-class joint. This may sound difficult, but keep in mind, they don't serve french fries even in a French restaurant.

Second, remember tea is a high-class drink, hot not cold. If you have trouble drinking tea, try picking open the bag with your extra fork to let out a few grounds. Then it resembles weak camp coffee.

Third, talk about high-class stuff. For instance, the conversation should be dominated by topics such as horses, salmon, and foxes, not mules, carp, and possums.

Fourth, drink everything with your little finger extended. Don't ask me why.

Last of all, hand everybody money. You've got eight or nine people in this place trying to make a living on one meal. If you can't afford to hand out greenbacks at every turn, just tell them you're taking care of them on the master bill. Then if you don't actually take care of them, wait at least a year before going back. Waiters have longer memories than do elephants, and a wounded elephant is no match for a stiffed waiter.

Well-informed, you now qualify to be well-fed.

But you say it looks like a lot of effort to eat in a high-class joint? And it sounds a bit stuffy? And who can afford it more than once or twice in every generation?

All good points. Maybe that explains why Dewey pulls his bass boat with a Lincoln.

Harbingers of Spring

Every spring they crop up—get-togethers of tradesmen and enthusiasts, swapping stories and selling each other gear and tackle they can't do without. Generally referred to as Boat Shows, the term belies the breadth of such expositions.

Everyone from tackle manufacturers to wildlife artists will be displaying their wares at these events. And outdoor associations will show up to promote their causes. For instance, you will find representatives from Quail Unlimited, Deer Unlimited, and Ducks Unlimited. At a show last year, I saw a display for Rabbits Unlimited, which doesn't sound like such a tough thing to accomplish as long as you have two to start with.

Although there is something at Boat Shows for the entire family, perhaps the ones who enjoy them the most are the kids. Mine go every year to tromp from booth to booth, stopping wherever there's candy or wild animals, proving once again that it's a world of eat or be eaten.

Part of the entertainment these shows provide are the funny characters you see. Dealers use everything from robots to people in chicken suits to attract attention. At one show, however, I got into trouble for pointing and laughing hysterically at a large round character with knobby knees. It turned out to be a security guard in shorts.

Some aspects of these shows make me nervous. I'm not bothered by the guns, knives, or motorized vehicles. What's scary is to take my kids to a place where you can buy so many raffle tickets for puppies. The Law of Averages says that sooner or later we might win one. Murphy's Law says we could win them all.

Art dealers and artists seem to be in cahoots with the dog rafflers. It's almost as if they're advertising for these fundraisers, because every print has at least one puppy chewing on a boot. But the prices for these prints are always reasonable, usually within a few dollars of what that boot cost *before* the puppy got it.

One scene at Boat Shows guaranteed to rattle your nerves is the fellow shaving with an ax to promote his sharpeners. I've always wondered what would bring a person to do that. Has he always used axes? Maybe he started out as a teenager using a hatchet, or he could be mellowing out, having cut back from using a chain saw.

As you can see, outdoor shows will expand your mental horizons.

Every year, the equipment on display gets bigger and better. Now it's hard to tell whether a large round tank is a baitwell for striper fishermen or a hot tub for an RV.

If you come to a Boat Show looking for new gadgets, you won't be disappointed. In fact, you can find lures that beep, blink, or rattle. Some have neutral buoyancy, neither sinking nor floating, but hovering at an intermediate level as if weightless. I'm not sure whether this tells us what NASA engineers do with their spare time, or why fishermen aren't asked to be astronauts.

A lot of gadgets that sneak into shows barely qualify as outdoor equipment. For example, at a recent show I saw one of those amazing vegetable choppers that slices and dices. I can't guess what this has to do with fishing, unless you can use one to cut chum into party shapes. It did, however, come with a free Ginsu Hook Sharpener.

Perhaps the strangest offerings at outdoor shows are the vitamins and food supplements. Talk about a tough sales job. I wouldn't list among the health-conscious a group that lives on Beanee Weenees, Vienna Sausages, and pork rinds.

Taxidermists also set up booths, showing off their award-winning mounts. Every year these animals look more lifelike. In fact, I was thinking about trying to get a wild boar mount for my living room. Not that I've ever taken a wild boar—I just relish the mental image I have of that being the first thing a burglar would see when he turned on his flashlight.

Besides all the commercial booths, many outdoor shows schedule special events to entertain the crowds. One of the most popular has a professional bass fisherman demonstrating the latest techniques, using a tank stocked with live fish. In every audience, there are a few skeptics who figure anyone could catch those fish. Not me.

I'd get so excited I'd flip the lure clear into the third row of the audience and give a whole new meaning to the term "jerk bait."

Another form of entertainment at these shows are the competitions, covering everything from photo contests to calling showdowns. And these competitions usually draw some amazing experts. At a turkey-calling event last year, I heard some turkey sounds so enticing that if performed in the field the hunter would have to shoot to protect himself.

Deer hunters can bring in their trophy racks to have them scored as well. Usually, it's during this process that hunters learn just how much antlers shrink as they cure. The worst case of shrinkage I've heard of occurred to a rack I saw at last year's show. During the scoring process, the hunter who owned the rack commented to an acquaintance, "Honest, Joe, you wouldn't believe how much these things shrink. Why, when I shot this one, the spread was three inches greater and he had two more points."

I figured, at that rate, two more years on the wall and that deer would be a spike buck.

Among the most popular events are the dog-training demonstrations. But after a few consecutive years of seeing retrievers perform, maybe a change would be nice. For instance, I'd really like to see how they train those TV wiener dogs to drag race.

At Boat Shows, you can talk to wildlife experts who are on hand to answer questions. Usually, the adults will ask them easy things like, "What's the state record for largemouth bass?" But it's the kids that ask the stumpers: "Do fish get the hiccups?" "How do salmon know their way home?"

The rehabilitated animals always draw a crowd. Among these critters are predatory birds that ran into windows, attacked concrete statues on a bird bath, or else are still recovering from attending past outdoor shows.

Believe it or not, you can also find boats at Boat Shows. These vessels have become specialized, like so much of our tackle. Now you can buy bass boats, walleye boats, even skiffs designed for shallow-water fishing. The only boat that's still hard to find is one for floating haphazardly while dunking worms.

(By the way, did you ever notice that nearly everything except boats can be demonstrated at a Boat Show? Sure, you can look at a boat's accessories, pick a color, even see if it's comfortable. But you still have to ask yourself, "Does this thing FLOAT?")

Even fancier than the boats at the show are the recreational vehicles. I admit, I walk through and covet these RVs, but I can always bring myself back to reality with a simple question, "Would I really be comfortable roughing it in accommodations fancier than my house?"

Of course, the answer is always "Yes." Too much reality can be a bad thing, even on a spring day at a Boat Show.

Fishing with Women

Lest some women's libber turns into Mombo and hunts me down with a curling iron, let me flatly state that this is not a sexist article. It is merely a reflection on certain sociological truths, collected and deliberated upon by one of the world's wisest individuals. Matter of fact, she's standing right behind me now offering encouragement.

I just wish she'd take it easy with the curling iron.

You might be surprised to learn that women began fishing with men hundreds of years ago, and their return to our lakes, streams, and oceans is merely a revival of this activity. Sociologists point to the design of ships as their evidence.

You see, the problem then as now is that women always catch more fish than do men. Early sea captains found this belittling, and being macho types, took matters into their own hands. At first, the women were tied onto ropes and lowered over the side for a few dousings to discourage them. To make this easier, sailors created wheels with handles to reel them in, thus the derivation of the term "winch," which came to be applied to both, though spellings may vary.

Even this failed to subdue their fishing prowess, so captains had women tied to a spar and hung out over the bow. Regular treatment like this finally did discourage women from fishing, say sociologists. Just to make sure they stayed discouraged, the captains carved wooden likenesses for their ships to serve as reminders. We now call these "figureheads."

These scientists thought at first that the revival of mixed fishing, men and women in the same boat, could clean up the sport and eliminate all the lying, swearing, and telling of coarse jokes that goes on. But this never happened, largely because men do these things, too. Sociologists have noted, however, the natural friction that continues between men and women in a boat and believe it still results from the natural phenomenon that women always catch more fish.

No one really knows why this happens. A few scientists, probably men, explain it as differences in hormones. Since most men know about as much about hormones as pigs do about fly-casting, even if this were true, it wouldn't matter because we wouldn't understand it anyway.

Another possibility is that women generally smell better. This scent gets on their bait and the fish like it. One of my buddies, Beanpole, tried to test this theory, mixing some of his Old Spice in with his Fish Formula. The resulting concoction was less than pleasant and in fact would have passed for baboon breath.

It didn't work.

Another buddy spent some time pondering this natural advantage of women, mostly because of the jeering he received at his bass club outings when his wife checked in with the biggest fish. He had a different theory. He attributed his wife's superior catch to her having more fishing time, thinking that while he drove the boat, stowed the gear, watched the sonar, and fretted over the pH, she just fished.

To test this hypothesis, he decided to fish with his shirt off to distract her. He learned two things. First, the trick didn't work, apparently because of excessive long-term ingestion of Beanee Weenees. His wife lost her appetite altogether, fished straight through lunch, and limited out. Second, he decided that January was a poor month for such an experiment.

Anyway, men should spend less time trying to understand this phenomenon and more time learning to live with it. Since I'm probably way ahead of most men in this area, having been outfished often by women, I'll offer a few tips.

First, if you give your spouse or girlfriend a fishing rod for Christmas, don't buy an Ugly Stik. They can read the fine print and might take it personal and get even. Being beaten is one thing; being humiliated in your own boat is another.

Likewise, if you get her some crankbaits along with the rod, just call them lures.

Develop a host of good excuses to use with the Bass Club. You can always try, "I was busy taking off her fish," "I put her over the honey hole," or if she's not around, "I really caught most of them."

Since all these guys have been outfished by a woman at one time or another, they will nod, smile knowingly, and pretend they actually believe you.

Men who cannot accept this demeaning experience also have some alternatives.

For instance, you could get even with the woman in your boat by leaving the lid up on the livewell. For some reason, this really drives them nuts.

As a last resort, you could revert to time-tested methods from the days of old. Actually, a bass boat doesn't look half bad with a figure-head.

Bringing Home a Pup

Besides love and companionship, a new pup can bring much into your home, things such as your neighbor's shoes, bits of garbage, and dead animal skins.

In return, you have the responsibility to give something back, particularly to your neighbor. But your dog deserves feeding, housing, and training, and these are just the basics.

To start on the right foot, you begin by picking the right pup for you. There are many theories on how to pick a pup. One is to pick out the biggest, most active pup in the litter. This makes little sense to me when the first lessons you teach him will be whoa, sit, and heel.

Some trainers suggest that you should not worry about the pup, but pick one from a litter with good parents, adding, "Fruit never falls far from the tree." There's some truth to this. Of course, my last pup chewed down the tree.

Prospective owners often debate the importance of getting a pup that comes with papers. All things being equal, I prefer pups with papers, particularly to put under them during the drive home.

When I pick a pup, for some reason I like to look at his teeth. I think subconsciously it's to gauge how many shoes he'll go through.

Every owner has different preferences in dogs. That may be why people say dogs often resemble their owners. The last pup we got did nothing but eat and sleep, which my wife says proves that theory.

My particular pup had big feet and a potbelly. After that wisecrack by my wife, I made it a point to suck in my gut and stand up straight. Unfortunately, so did the pup.

Many owners make the mistake of treating their dogs like children. Spoiling a dog is all too easy. One of my hunting buddies has a

Lab that won't make water retrieves unless he can flag down a passing boat.

Another sign that dogs are spoiled appeared on the market awhile back. It's a product called doggie ice cream. You know your dog is really spoiled if he won't eat it without hot fudge.

Whether they spoil their dogs or not, owners tend to brag about their pets. The worst example I have seen was a jeep with a bumper sticker that read, "My Pup Is A Terrific Dog At Penelope's School For Fine Pups."

Training is as much a necessity as feeding. If you train your dog yourself, there are several things you need to know. For instance, the three most important commands are sit, stay, and NOT ON THE CARPET!

Properly training your pup requires a number of tools. I bought mine in a kit that contained a training manual, a leash, and a small shovel.

I've read several training manuals, and they say the first thing to teach a pup is to come when called. How am I supposed to get a three-month old pup to do this when my kids won't?

Thinking I needed extra help, I took my dog to obedience school. Up until then, I never realized a dog could be sent back a grade.

Even after two months of class, my dog wouldn't retrieve. The closest he ever came to a retrieve was the day I bought him; he fetched a nice price for his former owner.

This particular obedience school was big on hand signals. Sometimes, I regret teaching my dog hand signals. You'd be surprised at some of the things he says.

Despite all your best efforts, count on your dog to embarrass you repeatedly. It got so bad for one of my hunting buddies that he put someone else's name and address on his dog's collar.

For instance, one day he brought his dog into my house, assuring me he was housebroken. I guess in a way he was right. As soon as the dog got inside he broke practically everything.

But then that's pretty normal. Even dogs like Lassie must have made mistakes in their younger days. I'll bet there was even an early show where June Lockhart said, "No, Lassie, when I said fetch a doctor, I didn't mean a proctologist."

That may be another reason dog is man's best friend. After the wife and neighbors are kept up all night by the barking, man and dog have no other friends.

It hardly seems fair that dogs only have one life, and cats have nine. Of course, it does explain why dogs run in packs. One cat can be split nine ways.

Of all the toys pups may have, old shoes are their favorites. I think it's because of the odor. Without getting out of the house, old shoes are as close as a pup can get to road-kill.

For some reason, dogs really like things that stink, and they often roll in the worst of them. Some animal behavior experts believe this is to cover their own scent and help them creep up on their prey. Either that or dogs consider this a good way to fend off small children.

With all the turmoil they create, you wonder how dogs ever convince you to bring them home. I guess it can be explained by the sad eyes, moist nose, and droopy tongue. I always give in when my kids do that.

In the end, even I got close to the pup. After all his barking and the neighbor's threats, it was either get close or not share the dog house.

Finding the Right Resort

You can easily find resorts perched on the edge of golf courses or lined with a bank of tennis courts. You might even be able to locate lodging with a health spa where you can be packed in mud, fed wild nuts, and made to row for hours on a boat that goes nowhere. (Although many outdoorsmen might have done those things at one time or another, they certainly didn't pay extra for the experience.) The trick is to find a resort that caters exclusively to the outdoorsman.

For starters, most hotels are located where outdoorsmen don't want to go, such as in large cities or near airports. When was the last time you got lost, came to the end of a gravel road, slid into the ditch, got stuck, then looked up to find yourself in front of a Marriott?

Most hotels are far too upscale for the average outdoorsman on safari. You can tell you're in the wrong place if the bellboy takes one look and tells you to drive around back to pick up the garbage.

Hotel chains even offer the wrong kinds of niceties to attract the average outdoorsman. For example, bathroom accessories usually include things like soap, shampoo, and lotion. You never check in and find free samples of Buck Lure, Fish Formula, and Deet.

Some modern hotels seem to go out of their way to remind you of your problems. The cable TV offers around-the-clock updates on world disasters, then first thing in the morning they personalize the news by sliding the bill under your door. What I'd really like is for my bill to be mailed home and a fishing forecast slipped under the door.

These same hotels provide plastic bags for overnight laundry service. Just once I'd like to drop my baitcaster in one of those bags to see if someone would oil it, pick out the backlashes, and return it with new line.

Even hotel food seems designed for someone other than outdoorsmen. Most of their menus have little symbols indicating "Heart Healthy" foods; what we really need is a symbol for foods that counteract the gastronomic disorders associated with eating out of cans for extended periods.

If you think about it, most hotels are planned for people who consider their lodging a key part of their vacation. Outdoorsmen, on the other hand, usually just come to hunt, fish, and otherwise stomp around. Most, in fact, would consider it a luxury to have over their heads a roof that doesn't leak.

Shuttle service from the hotel to the airport is a frivolous waste for outdoorsmen, who have no desire to go to an airport. Of course, it might be great to have hourly shuttle service to the bait shop.

Perhaps hotels could trade in their vans for four-wheel-drive vehicles with CB radios. Then, instead of carrying you to and from the airport, they could be winching you out of the mud.

Outdoorsmen are actually discouraged from staying at most hotels. Some establishments have policies that downright discriminate against us, rules such as "No dogs," or "No waders in the lobby." I once stayed in a hotel that had a sign in the room that read, "Don't clean pheasants in the bathtub."

Luckily, it was fishing season. I have since noticed that they now advertise scales in every bath.

Now, if a resort were to cater to outdoorsmen, it would stay booked and be outrageously profitable, mainly because outdoorsmen are so easy to please. Designing the ideal outdoor resort, therefore, would actually be quite simple.

For starters, the perfect outdoor resort would be cheap. A high-class place may pay someone to turn the sheets down for you, but at $14 a night, I'll bet you'd be willing to unzip your own sleeping bag.

The ideal hotel would be off the beaten path, so obscure you would never see a celebrity there, unless you include in this category the Orkin Man.

For sure, it wouldn't have a computer. Most hotels spend exorbitant amounts on systems that track your stays, credit them to an account, and after a certain number of visits allow you to cash them in for free lodging. These people don't understand human nature. Anyone spending that much time lounging around a resort needs to be kicked out and sent back to work before he loses his job.

Some slick marketers are beginning to recognize the need for resorts in the outdoors, so be on the lookout for impostors. Just recently, I heard one hotel trying to jump on the bandwagon with a radio ad aimed at outdoorsmen. You might have heard it, too. It ended with, "C'mon by, we'll leave the bug zapper on for ya."

It's a dead giveaway when these hucksters call their rooms by fancy names to disguise what they really are. For example, a "bungalow" is a cabin so small your Lab couldn't turn around in it. If they call it a "lodge," then there's probably no heat. And if they offer you a "loft," they've rented all the rooms and are putting you upstairs at the local fire department.

When they advertise double beds, this implies you get a mattress *and* box springs.

Individual climate control? Another fancy phrase they use. All it means is that the windows aren't nailed shut.

Usually pretty reliable, travel guide books won't always help. One resort I looked up had a puzzling little symbol by it that looked like a "plumber's helper." I didn't know whether that meant each room came equipped with one or that guests should bring their own.

Since it was the only hotel near the lake I wanted to fish, I booked a room there anyway. What a mistake. At check-in, I requested a wake-up call and the clerk handed me a rooster. Evidently I looked hungry because he also asked for a deposit.

Probably the only way you can screen out unacceptable resorts is to ask the proprietor if he likes to hunt and fish. If he says "Yes," then you'll know the food, room, and services are designed to suit an outdoorsman's tastes.

Of course, you can also bet that on any opening day, his inn will be closed.

Night-Fishing Tips

Most fishing advice concentrates on how or where to catch more fish. That's fine for daytime fishermen, but night fishermen need information on other topics like breathing inside a gnat cloud, getting lost in the fog, or playing possums on light tackle.

Weird stuff happens after dark. Fishermen run over logs, scare off skinny-dippers, hook bats, step off the ends of docks, pour coffee in their laps, eat bait, and on rare occasions, catch fish. Since catching fish takes only 2 percent of their time and all the other stuff takes 98 percent, smart fishermen adjust their tackle and techniques for night conditions.

The perfect rod for night fishing is six to seven feet long with a good backbone and a tip suitable for flipping snakes off the trail. The reel should have a good drag, but one that in no way resembles the wail of a rabid wildcat dropping kamikaze-style into your boat from a limb hanging just inches over your head, especially if your fishing partner is jumpy or has a full bladder.

Boats also require special preparation. For example, if you forget your drain plug in the daylight, you have a problem; forget it at night and you have a chance to converse with fish.

Radar would be nice for boats after dark, but it's impractical. Most fishermen simply slow down—they've learned that reaching out and touching a stump at 40 mph will connect them with more than Ma Bell.

Casting after dark presents additional problems, such as determining whether your lure has plopped onto water or land. This makes lure selection critical, especially regarding two features. First, you want a lure that splashes when it lands; otherwise you might unknowingly spend a lot of time fishing for possums. Second, just in case you do hit land, the lure should in no way resemble something a skunk might eat.

Many fishermen choose noisy lures just to keep track of them. Perhaps the all-time favorite is the black Jitterbug. Bass mug Jitterbugs. The soft gurgle of these lures carries a message of false bravado, like a kid whistling in the dark. Fishing Jitterbugs across a shallow point can be as effective as slow-trolling pork chops through a dog pound.

Lunar phases also play an important role in night fishing. In fact, nearly all fishing tables take the moon into account when predicting the most active feeding times of fish, and therefore, the best fishing periods. All animals supposedly follow feeding urges based on the moon. That might explain why the fish bite whenever I stop to eat.

These tables are so important that I always study them before night fishing trips. If a major feeding period is predicted, I pack a big meal; if it's a minor period, I only need snacks.

Night fishermen should also carefully plan what they're taking along for snacks. Experience has taught me not to pack pretzels if I'm fishing with worms. Always remember—things that crunch when the sun shines should still crunch at night.

Perhaps the most important skill a night fisherman can learn is knowing when *not* to take a closer look. If a stick resembles a snake, that should be good enough. Verifying this resemblance doesn't matter.

The same goes for eyes that reflect light. Lots of nocturnal animals have eyes. All of them, in fact.

Skunks, by the way, are part of this group.

The one nocturnal bandit whose eyes you won't notice is the bat. At the speed at which a bat travels, ultralight topwater lures apparently resemble large moths. Should you be so lucky as to hook a bat, you will instantly be more supportive of catch-and-release. At the very least, a hooked bat will help polish your skills with a net.

The bottom line on fishing after dark is that you have to stay alert. This may be the biggest problem night fishermen have. The chirp of crickets, the hum of jar flies, the gentle lapping of waves against the boat all lull me to sleep. To keep awake all night, I have to drink approximately one cup of coffee every hour. That might explain why the period after midnight is often referred to as the "wee hours."